C0-AVD-058

Parenting:

Ward and June Don't Live Here Anymore

Written by Jim Dugger
Edited by National Press Publications

NATIONAL PRESS PUBLICATIONS
A Division of Rockhurst College Continuing Education Center, Inc.
6901 West 63rd Street • P.O. Box 2949 • Shawnee Mission, Kansas 66201-1349
1-800-258-7246 • 1-913-432-7757

National Press Publications endorses non-sexist language. However, in an effort to make this handbook clear, consistent and easy to read, we've used the generic "he" when referring to both males and females throughout. The copy is not intended to be sexist.

Parenting: Ward & June Don't Live Here Anymore

Published by National Press Publications, Inc.
© 1991 National Press Publications, Inc.
A Division of Rockhurst College Continuing Education Center, Inc.

Printed in the United States of America

11   12   13   14   15   16   17   18   19   20

ISBN 1-55852-026-0

Table of Contents

1

PARENTING PATTERNS

Welcome to the wonderful world of parenting! Is that too gushy? Too sentimental? Too unbelievable? Then how about parenting is hard work spiced with great moments of pleasure? More realistic? Probably so. In fact, more than likely you have said to yourself at one time or another, "If I'd only known what I was getting into, I'd never have had kids." Don't feel guilty. That's a natural feeling because parenting is hard work. BUT it is not impossible. The type of parenting you may have grown up with, the type Donna Reed and the Cleavers made popular on television, is probably not the type of parenting you are experiencing. Today's families aren't the "black and white" families of the 50's TV show. We are, because of our options as adults and a society, multi-colored, technicolored families. What worked for Ward and June Cleaver, as you may have already found out, is woefully simplistic and inadequate for your family.

This guide is to give you ideas to help you cope with some of the problems parents face today. Although it is written with the working couple in mind, it is also useful for those of you who are single parents and even those of you in the traditional nuclear family.

Parenting Patterns

Some of you probably know exactly what type of parenting pattern
or style you are using. Others may be so new to the parenting scene
that you are still using the hit or miss method. Identifying parenting
patterns can be useful because it can open up communication between
you and your spouse concerning how you want to raise your children
and how you will respond to the problems that inevitably arise for you
as parents. The easiest way to think of parenting patterns is to think of
them going from one extreme to the other, from the adult-centered
family to the child-centered family. Most experts agree that the
farther you are from the middle, the more potential problems you may
experience.

Parenting Patterns

Adult-Centered		Balanced		Child-Centered	
Dictator Family	Benevolent Dictator Family	President's Council: Advise and Consent Family	Family Council Family	Egalitarian Family	Manipulative Family

Each of the above parenting patterns has distinct advantages and
disadvantages. The one you use is probably patterned after the family
you grew up in or is a reaction to that family's pattern. For example,
if you grew up in a very adult-centered family, you may uncon-
sciously choose to give your children more say in what happens in the
family.

The Dictator Family

Most of us can identify with this parenting pattern because this is
a very traditional way of parenting. In most of Western society, the
father is the boss. What he says goes. He may seek input from his
wife and traditionally later on from his eldest son, but ultimately he
makes the decisions. In the extreme form of the Dictator Family, the
father sees the children as having little worth. They are there to fetch
his slippers, pipe, etc. Children are to be seen and not heard. He
would not think of asking their opinions and, even as they become
adults, he still rules, thus the name Dictator Family.

He sets the standards and, if they cannot live up to those standards, some sort of punishment is doled out. Quite often this punish-

ment is physical, but it can just as easily be emotional or mental. Adult children are not physically punished. They are disowned for breaking the rules of the family. In some cases the family does a flip-flop from the traditional role and the mother calls the shots, quite often because of an early death of her spouse. Either way, the characteristics of this parenting style are the same.

The Advantages

- Everyone in the family knows his place. Rules are clearly understood.

- There is a sense of tradition.

- For the child who responds well to structure and sees the world in black and white, this style of parenting works well.

The Disadvantages

- Children are given little say in the rules that govern them and, consequently, some may rebel more than they normally would.

- This parenting style, unfortunately, lends itself to those parents who need to dominate and have power.

- Ultimately, the child suffers.

- Children grow up knowing how to follow rules but have little chance to think independently.

- Even adult "children" cannot escape from the head of the family until the father dies. Then the eldest son usually inherits the role as head of the family.

- Children and mothers are encouraged to find ways to sneak around the rules, form alliances against the head ("If you don't tell Dad, I won't either.") or resort to manipulative behavior to get their way.

The Benevolent Dictator Family

This is a variation of the Dictator Family. Dad (in most cases) is still the boss, but he's benevolent. He tries to consider the feelings and emotions of his family. He has some hard and fast rules which cannot be broken, but he is aware of what the family wants to do and bases his decisions on their wants and needs. He is likely to consult his wife and, in many cases, they rule equally as "head of the family." Many of you grew up in this type of family. Most of the families represented on television in the 50's were the Benevolent Dictator type. *Father Knows Best, Leave It To Beaver,* and *The Donna Reed Show* all operated under the Benevolent Dictator model.

The Advantages

- Children and spouse are given a chance to express their feelings without fear of reprisal.

- Society is comfortable with this style of parenting and supports it.

- There are probably more models for this parenting style than the others and it's easy to know what to do.

- All know their places in the family.

- Since the "dictator" is benevolent and is looking out for the best interests of the family, children tend to feel this type of family is a loving one.

The Disadvantages

- Women, because of their increasing role in society and the power structure, find themselves bosses in the office, but having little power at home.

- Since this model tends to make Dad the head of the house, this style of parenting can slight the girls in the family as they are relegated to a secondary position.

- The traditional type of teenage rebellion that most parents dread is bound to happen in this family because there is a central authority figure to rebel against.

The President's Council: Advise and Consent Family

The President's Council Family recognizes one person, usually the father or the mother and in some cases both of them, as the president, the one in charge. The remaining members of the family act like the president's council. They advise the president on important matters and give him or her their consent. They may even hold family meetings to exchange information. This is different from the Benevolent Dictator model because the president actively seeks the other family member's opinions. Children feel like they have a say in what happens in the family and, although the president doesn't always make a decision that everyone agrees with, the family knows they had a chance to present their side and argue their points. President's Council Families work well if the parents are fair-minded and respond to reasonable ideas and proposals. They attempt to allow children a say in the decision-making process based on the child's ability.

The Advantages

- All feel like they have a part in the family because they have some control over the decisions affecting their lives.

- The president does not have to be male. This lends itself to today's family which does not see itself as male-dominated.

- Independence and reasonable thinking are encouraged.

- Children are encouraged to think about decisions that affect them and argue for or against those decisions, thus giving them a feeling that their opinions have worth. This helps to build self-confidence.

- This environment helps children learn effective conflict management and negotiation skills.

- This style also lends itself to the variety of families we see today: the two-career family, the single parent family, the blended or step family and the extended family.

The Disadvantages

- Although everyone in the family has a chance to express opinions, it does not necessarily mean that their opinions will be enacted as a rule. If the president consistently overrules what the family wants, the system will start to fall apart. Since the president in the family is not elected, there could be a power struggle and possibly the ultimate breakup of the family.

- The structure is not as clearly defined. The person acting as president for some decisions, such as how money is doled out, may be different from the person who decides on social activities. For some children this can be very confusing.

The Family Council Family

This is true democracy in action. Those of you who have tried this form of parenting probably swear by it or swear at it. In its simplest form, the family meets on a regular basis, say once a week, and makes decisions ranging from how much allowance each child should get or whether or not to buy a new car, to what curfews should be. Usually one member of the family is elected to chair the meeting, but some families rotate this so each member has a chance. In some family councils, each person is allotted a number of votes depending on age or experience, thus giving the older members of the family more power. In other family councils, all family members have equal voting power after a certain age, but Mom and Dad have ultimate veto power. In some cases Mom or Dad is the official treasurer and if the family decides on something that is financially impossible, the treasurer has veto power. Some families even go so far as to have a constitution. Needless to say, this type of family takes time; but for those families that work at it, communication is excellent and the family tends to pull together.

The Advantages

- All members of the family have a say in what goes on and a vote on all decisions.

- Children learn to think and present their views.

- Children learn the democratic process they will use in their adult lives.

- The family is drawn together because they communicate regularly and because they have agreed to abide by the rules they have made.

- Rebellion is minimized because it is harder to rebel against the family than against one person. This is not to say that rebellion doesn't happen, however.

- Because the Family Council needs time to work, the family is forced to find time to meet, thus keeping communication open.

- This approach teaches skills such as negotiation, problem-solving, compromise and governing by consensus.

The Disadvantages

- The Family Council can take an immense amount of time and, with varying schedules, this type of structure may not work.

- Having all decisions made by the family is difficult for some adults. These adults will be uncomfortable giving their children that much "power."

- If the Family Council model is not started early in the family, it may be difficult to switch to this form, particularly if the family has had difficulty communicating or has been using a different parenting style. If you really want to move to a Family Council style, you should do so gradually.

The Egalitarian Family

This type of parenting might also be called the anarchy model because each family member is out for himself. This type of family usually evolves when the children have reached adolescence and young adulthood. Each member follows his or her personal set of rules. As long as those rules don't interfere with anyone else, the family runs smoothly. Since each member is treated more or less equally, there is no higher authority to appeal to if your "rights" are being violated. Mom and Dad gave up that authority when they went to this type of parenting. There is no family council because there is no need for one. Disagreements are handled through a variety of ways: force, alliances with other family members, manipulative behavior and "I'll-scratch-yours-if-you'll-scratch-mine" agreements. This type of parenting can work if everyone is mature. And that is why it is most likely found with families consisting of adolescents or young adults. It is also, unfortunately, the type of parenting some parents choose because they really aren't interested in taking on the responsibility of childrearing. In these cases, the children become "street-wise" at an early age or are emotionally abandoned.

The Advantages

- Allows mature children who want or need to make their own decisions the freedom to do so.

- There is little to rebel against because each child is making his/her own decisions.

The Disadvantages

- Young children can suffer from being given too much responsibility too soon and with little structure.

- This type of parenting becomes an easy out for many immature parents.

- Few families can function this way for very long.

- Because each family member is acting independently, the potential for conflict is greater in the family.

The Manipulative Family

At the opposite end of the spectrum from the Dictator Family is the Manipulative Family. Here the roles are completely reversed and the children in the family rule. In the truest sense of the word, this is a child-centered family. Whatever the children want is done. The parents live for their children and through their children.

The stereotypical "stage mother," the mother who pushes her child into acting or dance, is an example of the Manipulative Family. The child is manipulating the mother, and the mother is manipulating the child. She no longer has any life other than that of her child. This can also be seen in the sports fanatic father whose son or daughter is "pushed" into sports for Dad's glory. In other cases, little Johnny or Susie can do no wrong. As long as the family can afford the children's needs, this family will function.

However, in the long run a number of things will happen. When the children leave home, they will be in for a big shock when they discover the world doesn't revolve around them. Adjustment to adult life can be painful and quite often the "adult" child continues to ask Mom and Dad for both financial and emotional support. When either or both parents die, the "adult" child is forced to grow up overnight. Many do not make the transition. When the children leave home, their parents will suffer acutely from the empty nest syndrome. If they have devoted their whole lives to their children, many mothers find themselves in a deep depression when the last child leaves home.

The Advantages

- Initially, the children will feel totally loved.

- On the surface, parents can appear to society as good providers and loving parents.

The Disadvantages

- The children grow up with a false sense of power and unrealistic expectations.

- When the children leave home, they will not know how to function effectively in the outside world. They will not know how to interact with peers.

- These children grow up with an unrealistic, self-centered view of the world and possessions.

- These children, for all practical purposes, do not mature emotionally.

- When their parents die, these children are brutally introduced to reality because their benefactors are gone.

- When the last child leaves home, the parents suffer more from empty nest syndrome than any other parenting style.

The pattern you choose depends on many factors. Most parents choose a pattern similar to their own parents' pattern. When a couple from two varying patterns decide to have children and don't talk about how they will parent, problems can occur. As in any relationship, there are no hard and fast rules. Family dynamics affect how you relate to your spouse and children. Discussing parenting can help you and your spouse be better parents.

2

WHAT STAGE ARE WE IN NOW:
IDENTIFYING PARENTING AND CHILDHOOD STAGES

Stages in a Family

When we had our first child and were worried about whether what he was doing was normal, my aunt, who raised five children, always said, "It's just a stage. He'll grow out of it." Luckily, she was right. All of the parenting classes in the world could not have stressed enough that parenting is not just learning about one time such as babies, but is a series of stages a family goes through. By adopting my aunt's philosophy we got through many a "crisis" with our first child. When our second came along, we could at least identify the stages. And when the third arrived, we could not only identify them, we could also anticipate them and even enjoy them. Unfortunately, what my aunt failed to tell us was how to cope when our firstborn was going through his Preadolescence stage, and his sisters were in their School and Activities stage and the Big Step stage.

Parenting Stage	Children's Stage
"Isn't he or she the most beautiful child?": The newborn	Baby: ages 0-1

They walk, they talk: The toddler	Discovery time: ages 1-3
Educating the child: The preschooler	Formal discovery time: ages 3-5
"My little girl's going to kindergarten.": The kindergartener	The Big Step: ages 5-6
"My baby's in school.": The school-age child	School and activities: ages 6-10
"Oh yeah, make me.": The preadolescent	Emotional storms: ages 10-13
"When can I drive, work, drink...": The adolescent	The Teenage years: ages 14-18
Breaking away: The young adult	Young adulthood: 18-22
"Hi Mom, I'm home again.": The adult child	Adulthood: 22+

"Isn't He or She the Most Beautiful Child?": The Newborn

For first-time parents, this is one of the most glorious times. Fathers routinely act giddy upon the birth of their first child and mothers spend hours just looking at the baby. That child becomes the center of the universe for a short time, until Mom goes back to work, or a little brother or sister is born, or he or she learns to walk and talk. But briefly, the baby is the only thing you think about. With the new baby come new concerns and issues.

1. Knowing what to expect is a big concern. Unless you have had previous children, you will be unsure of what to expect. There are numerous books on the market devoted to how your baby will develop from age 0 to 12. Look under "childrearing" or "family" in your bookstore. Although dear Aunt Edith may mean well and she may be correct in her advice, for your peace of mind, read about it or ask your pediatrician or family doctor. For quick advice, many hospitals and public libraries have tape banks about various topics. Of course, you can always rely on Mom or Dad also.

2. *Babies are demanding.* They expect to be fed when they are hungry, changed when they are wet and held for physical contact. Because their little stomachs do not hold much food, their cries for food are real because their stomachs hurt. As they grow older you will be able to stretch out their feedings. For all practical purposes, your life will become baby-centered for the first year of the baby's life. This is not to say that you won't be able to do anything else, but most parents who are working find during the first year they work and they take care of the baby. To cope with this you should:

- Set up a routine that all of you can live with. If you choose not to breastfeed, then decide who will take which feeding in the night. Parenting is an equally shared responsibility. June Cleaver could take all of the feedings because she was a full-time "housewife," but a working mother cannot be expected to bear the full responsibility for childcare. Decide who will take the baby to your childcare and who will pick him or her up.

- Cut back on your social engagements until the baby gets older. This is not to say you shouldn't do anything socially, but pare back for the time being.

- Do take time for yourselves. Go on a date occasionally without the baby.

- Establish a support system. This is described further in Chapter 7.

- Set priorities.

3. *Plan for the future.* With the arrival of the baby it is time to review your will (or have one drawn up) and your life insurance needs. Decide who will be your child's legal guardian if something should happen to you and your spouse. If you don't, the court will if the situation arrives.

4. *Guilt is a problem most new parents face,* particularly the mother. Well-meaning friends and relatives will make you feel guilty about your working, with innocent comments like, "Oh, how can you leave him? He's so precious." If you are at all uncertain, these comments can tear you apart. To weather the guilt that is sure to come, anticipate it and be prepared to answer it head-on. The decision to work is yours. Many a new mother, raised to have a

career, has gone stir crazy after a few weeks with a newborn and few adult contacts. Remember, guilt is a mind game you do not have to play.

5. *Loneliness is another problem* facing many new mothers, and a few fathers who elect to take a childrearing leave. It is important for the mother or father who stays home to continue to keep in contact with those he or she works with and what is going on in the workplace. Social outings with or without the baby should be planned. The first "showing" of the baby to those at work can be exciting, but don't be surprised if the initial excitement only lasts briefly. Your co-workers have work to do and will only "ooh" and "ah" for a short time before they have to get back to work. Keep such a visit short and plan to go back to visit without the baby later. You also need to have time away from the baby so you do not feel completely consumed by the baby. Arrange for your spouse to watch the baby while you go out with friends or back to the office for a visit. Hire a competent babysitter and escape the world of diapers and spit-up for your own sanity.

6. *Spoiling is another concern* of new parents and is certainly a concern of new grandparents. You will find your parents will probably be more concerned about you spoiling the baby than you are. It is difficult to spoil a newborn. The issue of spoiling comes as the child becomes mobile and starts to talk. You will spoil your children if you give them everything they want, when they want it. The older the child, the less instant gratification he or she needs. If you work at keeping communication open and expect your children to take responsibility for their actions, they will not be spoiled. My mother-in-law put it succinctly when our first child arrived. "Remember, he came to live with you, not you with him."

7. *Toward the end of year one your child will start crawling.* A child needs a chance to safely explore. Although playpens are great for parents, they do little for helping a child learn. It is better to restrict movement as little as possible. A child learns by exploring, and as he or she gets older, he or she will ask you questions about what he or she has discovered. A friend of ours described her messy house as an educationally rich home. She had the right attitude.

8. *Language development for some parents becomes a concern* because they want their child to get a headstart for a good education. During the first year, it is important that you talk to your child and

read to him or her. The baby is learning the cadence of the language, its intonations and rhythm. By the end of the first year it is normal for the baby to make sounds that, though they do not sound like any actual word, do have the distinct cadence of the parent's language.

9. *A final concern is childcare itself.* This is discussed more fully in Chapter 7.

They Walk; They Talk: The Toddler

Every parent anxiously awaits their child's first word and first step, and within a month of the child starting, you wonder why you ever wished such a thing to happen. This is a discovery time for the toddler and, like it or not, part of this stage is discovering the world by putting it in his or her mouth. It's natural for the toddler and frustrating for the parent. Whereas the baby's world is its crib and room, the toddler's world is made up of the whole house, the backyard, and any place he or she can run to before a parent catches him or her. It is a world of looking up at things: table tops, chairs, tall people, and for some even the dog.

The toddler is also discovering the world of words and their power. Many a swearing parent is reformed overnight when he or she hears the same words coming from the toddler's mouth.

Home safety becomes an issue:

- This is a time to put away valuables that can be broken unless you really do want to teach the toddler to just look, not touch.

- Books and magazines are best put up because page ripping is normal at this age.

- Cupboard doors should be latched. There are ingenious devices available; although my mother always seemed to fool her grandchildren with a spoon through the handles.

- All poisonous substances and drugs should be locked away and be put out of reach. (You may want to put guards on your electrical outlets.)

- Take time to explore the world with your toddler and read to him or her.

- Listen politely when the daycare worker or babysitter gushes about your child's first word or first step. Every working parent knows that the first word or step your child says or does when you're with them is THE important one. The others were mere dress rehearsals for Mom and Dad.

- Finding time for your toddler can be frustrating because his or her bedtime may be so early that you have little time to spend with him or her. As with the baby, establish a schedule that works for everyone in the family.

- Childcare is also an issue to be dealt with. This is discussed more fully in Chapter 7.

- It will also be during this time that your child not only learns what you mean by the word "no," but also learns to use "no." This is natural. Piaget, a child psychologist, describes the "terrible twos" as the time when the child learns that he or she has an ego and is a separate entity from his or her mother. This can be frustrating because you can spend endless hours in power struggles over needless issues. There is little to be gained, for example, in "fighting" with your two-year-old over what shirt he or she is wearing. It is more productive to turn the "dressing" into a game such as who can get dressed the fastest. Children at this age are easily distracted and a favorite toy to play with can take their minds off of what a moment ago they were so adamantly against.

- You will also be introduced to a new event during the toddler stage: the temper tantrum. Once again, it is normal. Don't reinforce the tantrum by giving it any more attention than it warrants. For example, if the child is screaming, ignore the screaming and go on with what you were doing. If, however, the child is banging his or her head against the wall, move the child to the sofa and let him or her bang away. The most difficult time to deal with a tantrum is in a public place or when others are around. In that case, remove the child from the attention-giving public. The time that this takes is well worth it in the long run. If the child gets attention with a temper tantrum in a public place, you many never get any shopping done. Rest assured, the crying will eventually stop.

Educating the Child: The Preschooler

For many parents the formal education of their child begins before he or she goes to preschool, with many teaching him or her to read as soon as is possible. There is concern among educators and psychologists that this rushing of education is damaging to children because they don't have time to be children. Most recommend age three as the earliest that a formalized education begins. While as the parent of a toddler you were concerned with a world that was basically around your home, now you need to be concerned about preschools and which is the best for your child. Your preschooler's world will also expand to include people you don't know, and may include not only the preschool, but field trips to exotic places like the fire station or the grocery store. Choosing a preschool can be a mind-boggling task. It needn't be.

- Ask other parents of preschoolers or kindergarteners which preschool they would recommend. Listen carefully to what they say. Do they have an axe to grind or a pet philosophy that clouds their opinion? For example, if they keep gushing about how that preschool has the largest percentage of eventual college graduates, they may be more concerned about looking good than they are about their child's education.

- If you can get time off, visit the preschool. Would you feel comfortable in the atmosphere?

- Talk to the teachers. Express your concerns. If your child is sick, for example, find out what emergency plans they have.

- If you can take your child with you to visit, do so and then ask him or her what he or she liked about the preschool.

- Decide what you want your child to gain and then match the preschool with the child. Some stress socialization, some academics, and some exotic curriculum like French and manners.

- Plan ahead. Many parents submit applications to preschools 12 to 24 months before their child is ready to attend. Start investigating schools early and find out what their enrollment and screening procedures are.

Another concern many parents of preschoolers have is that of aggression. One reason for aggression is having to learn how to share.

Toddlers and preschoolers are naturally selfish and sharing is an unnatural activity. "Mine" is a favorite word and is usually said emphatically. Although you may not be able to get your toddler or preschooler to share instantly, you still should not tolerate aggressiveness such as hitting or biting. Don't be tentative with the toddler or preschooler. They will understand a specific command much better than if you try to explain why they can't be aggressive. In other words, it's better to say, "No hitting" than to say, "We don't hit because we must learn to share." Save the explanations for later.

A highly emotional situation for some parents, commonly introduced when your child is a preschooler, is sexual play and exploration. It is natural and to be expected. Though you may be tempted to fly off the handle if you find your four-year-old son and your neighbor's four-year-old daughter examining each other's body, you will do much less damage psychologically by underplaying the situation. Encourage the children to play some other game, one they particularly enjoy. You may also want to use the situation as a time to answer questions your child may have about his or her body. The same is true about masturbation. It is natural and, although a taboo subject in many parts of society, it is likely that at some time you will need to deal with the subject. It is a good idea to discuss how you are going to respond to the situation prior to it happening. Many parents simply say, "Although there is nothing wrong with it, it is a private activity." There has been more damage done by parents overreacting than by the child actually masturbating.

"My Little Girl's Going to Kindergarten": The Kindergartener

After preschool, kindergarten is a piece of cake, right? Not necessarily, at least for the parent. Major decisions come with the child entering kindergarten. For some stay-at-home mothers and house husbands, the child's entry into kindergarten signals a return to the workforce. For other parents the concern is whether the child is ready for kindergarten. There is a great deal of pressure put on the child and parent by society during this stage. Once the child turns five, people start asking, "Are you going to kindergarten next year?" But five is not an age that every child should start kindergarten.

- If the child's birthday is in June, July or August, you may want to wait until the child is six to start kindergarten.

- If the child is small for his or her age and has a summer birthday you may want to wait.

- If the child is a boy and has a summer birthday, you may want to wait.

If you're unsure, visit your kindergarten without your child and talk to the teacher. Many school districts also have screening tests available to help you decide. Some even have a pre-kindergarten along with the regular kindergarten.

Most of the problems you may run into with the kindergartener other than the adjustment to a new school will be discussed in the following section.

My Baby's in School: The School-Age Child

Many parents feel that the hardest part of parenting is over when their children are finally in school all day. After all, the children can look after themselves, dress and feed themselves. What more could a parent want? Unfortunately, as in any other stage there are potential problems. It is not uncommon during this stage for parents to deal with lying, fears, sexual play, bad language, baby talk and bed wetting. Luckily, it is the rare child that has all of these problems, and most children have none at all. Here are ways to handle each of these situations:

1. *Lying.* Lying is usually indicates a larger problem. If your child occasionally tells a little white lie, you mainly need to confront him or her and follow through on some sort of consequence for telling the lie. Facing the Music as described in Chapter 6 is an effective method. If the child is a chronic liar, you should seek professional help. Talk to your family doctor for names of professionals who deal with child psychiatry.

2. *Fears.* It is natural that children experience fears. These quite often are in the form of nightmares. If you know that your child is experiencing fear, talk to him or her privately and assure him or her that having fears is normal. Try to analyze the reason for the fear. For some children, just talking about fear is enough to eliminate it. If the fear is controlling your child's life, seek professional help.

3. *Sexual play.* The same techniques as discussed in the pre-schooler's section of this chapter work at this age.

4. *Baby talk.* Although this is a limited problem, for some parents it becomes an overriding problem. Children usually revert to

baby talk because they want to delay growing up. Baby talk is also used by some as a way of identifying with a peer group. If baby talk is used to delay growing up, talking to your child about how he or she feels about growing up is a starting place. If you feel you cannot solve the problem, seek professional advice.

5. *Bed wetting* can be an embarrassing problem for the child and needs to be handled delicately rather than with ridicule. Since it is usually a physical or neurological problem, it is wise to talk to your family doctor or pediatrician. If it is an occasional problem, it may be that the child was overly tired when he or she went to bed and was unable to get up to go to the bathroom.

Quality Time Versus Quantity Time

There is much fuss about quality time versus quantity time for working parents. Don't get hung up on labels. *Kids aren't looking for quality or quantity, they're just looking for time with you.* Sometimes that involves interaction, but other times it's just being in the same room with you. Find time to be with them. Even though activities, clubs, sports and lessons take up a lot of time, they also mean spending a lot of time in the car if you live in suburbia, small towns or rural areas. That's good. Time in the car can be valuable communication time. There are no phones (unless you have a car phone) or televisions to interrupt you.

"Oh Yeah, Make Me": The Preadolescent

The ages of 10 to 13 can be one of great emotional storms. The calm little child that was the apple of your eye may at one moment tell you that you are the greatest parent in the world and at the next moment say, "I hate you." Puberty is a cruel trick that mother nature plays on children and their parents, and preadolescence is part of that trick. Preadolescent children are trying to cope with the hormones that are exploding in their bodies, while Mom and Dad expect unreasonable things like acting their ages. Peer pressure is also a factor. Friends become more important than family during this time. That's the bad news. The good news is that if you've given your child a strong value system and you keep loving them in spite of this phase, they will sift through the bad friends and arrive a few years down the road as perfectly well-adjusted young adults. Preadolescence and adolescence is like learning to ride a bicycle. There are a lot of spills and uncontrollable swerves. Sometimes Mom and Dad have to hold onto the bike and other times they run along beside, but eventually the child learns to balance and takes off on his or her own. Here are some tips on coping with the preadolescent.

- Listen carefully to what your child has to say.

- Don't instantly judge his or her friends and activities. In many ways his or her life at this age is similar to yours at the same age. But in other ways it is vastly different. For example, when you were 13, you were probably concerned about the opposite sex; however, you never had to worry about AIDS. Your pre-adolescent is vastly more knowledgeable about sex than you probably were, thanks to the media and sex education courses.

- If you feel strongly about certain issues, state those issues to your child. Set limits of key issues but be willing to give in on others.

- Your child will test you with statements such as, "I think I'll be a bartender when I grow up," when he or she knows full well that you expect him or her to go to college. Don't overreact.

- Weather the emotional storms by remaining calm. Remember, it's bad enough having one preadolescent in the family.

- Get to know your child's friends, but don't expect them to accept you as anything but your child's parent.

- Even though you find their music barely tolerable (nothing like Elvis or The Birds or Mick Jagger), take time to listen and learn some of the names of the groups and songs they sing. You'd be surprised what an impact that can make.

- Communicate in a way that works for both of you and keep the communication lines open.

"When Can I Drive, Date, Work, Drink...": The Adolescent

Teenagers are the best of times and the worst of times. It helps to understand that it is natural that teenagers rebel. They are trying to understand and define their world. Unfortunately, Mom and Dad and all they hold dear are what most teenagers rebel against. If there is ever a time you need to be sure of what you believe and why, it's when you have a teenager. You will be tested again and again.

Like preadolescence, the emotional storms will continue, but as your teenagers grow older they will have fewer and fewer storms. Boyfriends and girlfriends will come and go. As my aunt with five children says, "After the first two kids and all their 'romances,' I stopped getting excited about the new 'romance' until they announced the wedding plans." Parents of teenagers have to walk a tightrope of being interested in their teenager's life without appearing to be snoopy, the ultimate sin against a teenager.

Everything in a teenager's life will be a crisis. If you know that, then it's much easier for you as a parent to sort out what really is a crisis and help your teenager cope with it. Personally, I never thought of pimples as being a crisis, but to my teenage daughter they can be just as earthshaking as losing a boyfriend.

Teenagers are also paranoid. They are convinced that everyone is looking at them. That is normal. You may find that where you used to be acceptable (though old) to your preadolescent, you may now be unacceptable and archaic to your teenager. They may not want to go places with you because you embarrass them. Don't take it personally. This too will pass and you will be rediscovered in a few years, as the wonderful person you are.

When, when, when seems to start every sentence of the teenager's conversation with his or her parents. "When can I drive?" "When can I start dating?" "When can I have a part-time job?" "When can I drink?" "When can I...?" One of the reasons they ask these questions is to find out how you feel about these issues. You decide and set limits. Teenagers won't always like your answers, but if they seem reasonable they will probably abide by them. If, however, you use the argument— "Everyone is doing it," or "Because I said so"— be prepared for a battle. After all, you don't accept that argument from them. Teenagers are acutely aware of the ironies of the world and can be quite cynical. If you preach,"Do as I say but not as I do," you can expect trouble. Remember, you are their first and foremost role model. They will experience pressure from their peers, but the foundation of values you provide them with will help them decide what is right and wrong.

Specific issues such as drugs and alcohol abuse are discussed in Chapter 6.

Breaking Away: The Young Adult

This period for son and daughter and parent is a transition period. For many it means living at home while getting that first job. For others it means going away to college but living at home on the vacations and in the summer. Yet for others it means joining the service and coming home on leave. For you as a parent it means redefining your relationship from parent to equal adult. You may feel guilty because you can hardly wait for them to move out, but at the same time when they do, you miss them dearly. Issues at this time revolve around:

1. *Money:* Who's paying for college? Could I loan money to my son or daughter for a down payment on a car? Should I send him or her money so he or she can come home for the holidays? Who pays is based on financial ability and your own personal beliefs. Many believe that once their children become 18, they are on their own. Others believe they are obligated to put their children through college.

2. *Acceptable behavior:* Even though you are legally an adult you are still living at home and we are supporting you. What amount of control do you have over your child? Communication is the key here. If you are treating your "child" like an adult and he or she expects to be treated like an adult, then adult behavior can be expected. Adults do not mooch. They carry their own weight. You should have the same expectations for your adult children in your home as you have for any other adult in your home.

3. *Grades:* This is usually an issue when you are paying for the education and the grades are poor.

4. *Boyfriends or girlfriends:* How serious is this relationship? Is he or she good for my child? Is marriage and in many cases living together a possibility? Is my child sexually active, and if so, is he or she being responsible? Once again, communication is the key. These are issues that need to be discussed between parents and children. You may not agree with everything your child says or does, but you should respect his or her opinion. If, for example, your son wants to bring his girlfriend home for the holidays and sleep in the same room with her and you don't approve of this behavior, you need to tell him so. If you have kept the communication lines open, this will not be a problem. You do not have to accept everything your "child" does. Remember, he or she sees himself or herself as an adult. Treat him or her as such and you are more likely to get adult behavior.

5. *Drugs and alcohol:* How much control or influence do we as parents actually have? How do I know if there is a problem and once I identify the problem, what can I do about it? This issue is discussed further in Chapter 6.

"Hi, Mom, I'm Home Again": The Adult Child

One of the phenomenons of our time is the adult child who returns to live at home after being out on his or her own. This is almost always for financial reasons, usually when he or she is between jobs or going back to college. Sometimes it is also for emotional reasons after a divorce or major break-up with a boyfriend or girlfriend. Just when Mom and Dad could enjoy their retirement or their financially secure years, in pops their adult child to stay where board and room is free. Ben Franklin said that fish and visitors smell after three days. As much as you love your children, short visits are better than long stays.

- Establish with your returning child the exact length of stay and stick by your calendar.

- Sit down with him or her and realistically explain your financial situation if you really can't afford to have him or her live with you.

- Establish the ground rules you are comfortable with. This does not have to come off sounding like you're the parent and he or she is the child. Treat it more as, "This is what I expect of anyone staying at my home." If you don't let people smoke in your home, then stick to your guns. If you don't want him or her smoking in the house, he or she may not be happy, but will know where you stand.

- If he or she is working, expect him or her to help financially. There is nothing that moves children on more quickly than when they have to help "pay the rent."

- If he or she isn't working, expect him or her to help around the house or the yard. Have him or her earn his or her keep. As adults we are expected to be responsible and pay our way. For most young adults, this isn't a problem; but for a few it can be.

Combining Stages

Probably the real test of parenting is combining the various stages. It is quite possible that you could have one adolescent, a preadolescent, a school-age child and a preschooler, all at the same time. Interestingly enough, *the last child seems to determine the stage the family is in.* If you waited until you were in your 30's to start your family, you are still considered a young family, not because of your age, but because of your children's age. Last year we passed into a total teenage or adolescent family with our youngest turning 11. We are no longer concerned with Barbie Dolls and inexpensive toys for Christmas. Now there is nothing on the gift list under $50 because teenagers' "toys" are more expensive. We went on vacation and experienced five distinct opinions on what we should see and do rather than "This is what we are doing today."

But as my aunt says, "It's just a stage they are in," and sooner than we might like, we will be in another stage.

3

CREATING A VALUE SYSTEM

Each of us has our own value system and each family is a combination of the value systems both parents bring to the family. About 15 years ago Values Education was a hot topic in the schools. Many of you may have taken part in a values clarification class. Although Values Education is not currently the hot topic, it is helpful, however, if you and your spouse take time to discuss the values you want for your family. Don't assume you and your spouse have the same values.

The Values Spectrum

There are many terms that are used when talking about values. The values spectrum may help you define where your values lie.

RADICAL	Wants to change most things, even if it requires force.
LIBERAL	Embraces the new and is willing to discard the old.
MODERATE	Willing to change, but moves slowly.
CONSERVATIVE	Prefers to conserve the past.
REACTIONARY	Wants to return to the old days.

The values spectrum can deal with almost any situation from religion to politics to parenting. For example, Democrats tend to be liberal or moderate politically, while Republicans tend to be moderate or conservative. Fundamental and evangelical churches tend to be conservative to reactionary, while the large protestant denominations tend to be moderate and sometimes even liberal. Individual values tend to fall primarily into one of these categories. But it is possible to be moderate, for example, in all areas but one and to be quite liberal in that area.

If you really want to make an extensive study of values as a parent and see where you fall on the values spectrum, you can get one of the many books on values clarification and go through the exercises. Most of you, however, do not have time. Make a list of topics that you feel strongly about and discuss those with your spouse. The time taken is well worth it. You and your spouse may have totally different outlooks on the subject. Here are some of the standard topics and questions to get you started.

1. Child Rearing

- Who has primary responsibility for child rearing in your family or is it shared jointly?

- Do you believe in spanking?

- Who should do the disciplining?

- Do you believe in positive reinforcement when the child does something good?

- Whose responsibility is it to teach the child about sex?

- How do you instill values in your children?

- When should you start your children's formal education: preschool, kindergarten, at birth?

- How do you feel about boys playing with dolls and girls playing with trucks?

- How much television should your children watch?

- What kinds of friends do you want your children to have?

2. Your Child's Future

- How much education should you encourage or expect?

- What do you want your child to be when he or she grows up?

- Should you start some sort of financial plan to help your children in the future?

- How are you going to feel when your child doesn't want to lead the type of life you had hoped and expected?

- Should you have different expectations for your sons than for your daughters?

3. Church and Religion

- What kind of religious education do you want your children to have?

- Will your children have a formal religious education and attend classes in a Sunday School, parochial school, Hebrew school?

- Will you as a family be active in a formal religion?

- How will you feel if your child rejects your religious views?

- If you don't have strong religious views, how will you feel if your child becomes religious?

Discussing these and other topics will help you and your spouse explore your values as a family. Remember, you are attempting to define your family values. This doesn't mean you will always agree, but if you discuss and keep communication open you will understand what you agree on and where there are potential problems.

Looking at Your Parents' Values

Perhaps you have already discovered that your parents and your in-laws differ in values, particularly when it comes to parenting. That is normal. Parenting techniques and practices go through fashions just like clothing. And we all know that values change. In fact, psychologists and others call the clash of values the generation gap. You can come to an understanding of your own family's value system by looking at your parents' and in-laws' value systems. Take the same list of questions and try to answer them as your parents and in-laws would. If you're brave and they're cooperative, ask them the same questions. You may be pleasantly surprised at their answers.

The Church's Solution

Each religion also operates on its own value system; some are more conservative than others. Your choice of religion or lack of religion is one of America's great freedoms. When discussing your values and the ones you as parents want for your children, you may also want to look at the values of the religion you belong to. If you are not actively involved in a religion but your parents were, ask yourself what was it that you agreed with or disagreed with in that religion. Those answers are part of your value system. For example, if you stopped going to church or synagogue because you didn't feel you had to be in a building to worship God, perhaps one of your values is that you do not value formalized organizations.

Society's Values

Some people live in conservative communities while others live in liberal communities. Each community, whether it be local, state or national, has its own value system. These are expressed in its laws. Most laws in the United States are based on Judeo-Christian values, those found in the Jewish and Christian faiths. Another way to understand your values as a parent is to discuss those laws that you strongly agree or disagree with in your state or in the country. Take a look at the values spectrum and see where you fit. Where does your spouse fit?

Three Types of Value Systems

You have looked at a values spectrum. Now examine your philosophy of life. Don't let the word philosophy scare you off. The way you respond to situations, the way you live is your philosophy. One way to think of philosophy is to see it as a closet rod where you hang a set of values that keep your life organized. Without a philosophical rod you may not be sure who you are. There are three broad types of philosophies.

1. Idealist
2. Realist
3. Pragmatist

Idealists

The idealist has a set of values and expectations to measure the world by. If you are an idealist, you may say that all people are basically good. When something happens to prove you wrong, you do not change your values, you simply say, "All people are basically good, even though that one wasn't." In other words, you continue to use the same set of standards, no matter what. Idealists are often frustrated with the world because it doesn't measure up to their standards. Many perfectionists are idealists.

Realists

Realists take the world for what it is. Their expectations and values are based on reality. They have standards, but their standards are based on the world around them. For example, as a parent faced with trying to teach children about sex, the realist will more than likely take the view that their children will probably engage in premarital sex because that is statistically true. From that view of reality the realist parent will decide what to teach the child.

Pragmatists

The pragmatist has a sliding set of values based on the situation. He is the great compromiser. Pragmatists usually start out with a realistic view of the world and base their values on that, but if the situation changes, the pragmatist feels comfortable changing also. For example, if the pragmatist can see a good reason for changing his or her stance, he or she has no trouble doing so.

The Three Philosophies Compared

Let's take a sample situation and compare the three philosophies. Which do you and your spouse feel most comfortable with?

Your 16-year-old daughter comes home and says that she and her friends are going to a party on Saturday evening and asks your permission to drive the family car. You agree and set a curfew. She arrives home an hour and a half after her curfew. This is the first time she has ever broken a curfew that you set. She explains that though she was not drinking, one of her friends was, and she had trouble getting the friend to go home. The girl jumped out of the car and refused to get back in for about 45 minutes. Your daughter knew she should call to let you know that she was going to be late, but because of the friend and her jumping out of the car, a call was impossible. What would you do?

- *The idealist* would punish her for breaking the curfew, no matter what the reason was for breaking it. If breaking the curfew meant grounding for a week then the daughter would be grounded. The idealist's world tends to be black and white and the daughter should have stayed within the confines of that world.

- *The realist* would probably punish the daughter, but the punishment might not be as harsh because of the reality of the situation. The realist would be aware that there are times one cannot make curfew. This was one of those. If the realist has a value system that stresses helping friends, then the daughter would be forgiven. If the realist has a value system that stresses choosing friends carefully, then the discipline might be stronger.

- *The pragmatist* would listen to the daughter's story and more than likely not punish her, at least not for breaking curfew. The pragmatist would say that the situation required a judgment call by the daughter and the call was appropriate. The daughter, however, could still be disciplined for not calling if the pragmatist felt the daughter had ample opportunity to call or could have had another friend call. It all depends on the situation.

Each of us operates under a philosophy that we have learned and adopted. The major ones are the idealist, the realist and the pragmatist. The easiest way to remember them is:

— The idealist says, "This is the way it should be."

— The realist says, "This is the way it is."

— The pragmatist says, "It depends."

Helping Children Handle Tough Ethical or Moral Decisions

Naturally, the easiest way to help children handle tough ethical and moral decisions is to prepare them before they face the situation.

- Decide on a value system early in your parenting.

- Teach your child your value system.

- Play a game such as <u>Scruples</u> that gives you a chance to discuss situations that may call for your child to make a tough decision.

- Discuss tough ethical and moral decisions with your children at an appropriate age level. For example, discuss lying and stealing at a younger level, premarital sex at an older level.

- Keep communication lines open. This is one of the hardest things to do.

- Discuss why you believe what you believe.

- Decide if you want your child to have some sort of religious education. This could be anything from being actively involved in a church, going to Sunday School, or enrolling your child in a parochial school.

- Go through the exercises found in values clarification books with your children and discuss how you answer the questions and why.

Controversial Topics

It is difficult to escape controversial topics, and your children will be much more aware of those topics than you ever were in your childhood. This can be directly attributed to television and radio. Topics that previously were taboo in the media are discussed frankly. Your ability to discuss these topics with your children will depend on many things.

- Your own comfort level with the topic.

- Your set of values.

- Your philosophy about discussing controversial topics and whether your child should be informed or taught about those.

- Your knowledge of the topic.

- Your feelings on whether you, the schools, or your church should be teaching your children about the subject.

However, no matter what your stance, your child will, at some time, be exposed to the controversial topics of the day. In preparation, you and your spouse might discuss how you are going to handle particular subjects as they come up or as you bring them up. Even this process can be painful to some parents because their own upbringing and value system placed the topics off limits. Some of the "hot" topics of the day are as follows. What is your position on these and why?

1. **Abortion**—are you pro-life or pro-choice, or does it depend on the situation? At what point should your children learn about abortion?

2. **Euthanasia**—mercy killing. Does a person have a right to indicate when he or she wants to die in a terminal illness situation?

3. **Nuclear Armament**—or disarmament. Should we completely ban nuclear arms or do we need to simply reduce the number?

4. **Homosexuality**—Should homosexuals have the same rights as heterosexuals? How do you teach your children about homosexuality and what do you teach them?

5. **Drugs and Alcohol**—What should you teach your children about drugs and alcohol? Do you differentiate between "legal" drugs and "illegal" ones? What do you know about drug abuse and alcoholism?

6. **Birth Control**—Should schools dispense birth control? What do you teach your children about birth control in light of the large percentage of people who engage in premarital sex and the campaigns for safe sex?

7. **Sex Education**—Who do you want to teach your children about sex: you, the schools, the church? Or should they learn about it on their own? If it is taught in the schools, do you know what they are teaching? Do you agree or disagree?

8. **AIDS**—Who should be responsible for teaching your children about AIDS?

Teaching Children the Value of Money

Although not nearly as controversial as sex education, a practical value that all parents are faced with is teaching their children about money. If you do not bring up the subject, your child will. And sooner or later you will need to make some decisions about money and your child.

Allowances

Most child-rearing experts agree that giving a child an allowance is a good idea so your child has a chance to control some money, with little or no strings attached. An allowance will help foster independence in a child. The amount varies from family to family depending on the child's age, the family's financial situation and the times. However, don't base your child's allowance on your allowance as a child. An appropriate allowance in your day would probably not even "squeak" by today. For example, if you received 50¢ a week and a can of soda cost 10¢ in your day, then your child would need to receive $2.50 a week just to keep the same standard of living you had!

- Most experts indicate that allowances should not be attached to chores the child does. No one pays Mom or Dad to do the dishes so the child should learn that chores are just part of what a family does.

- Allowances should be based on age. It would be inappropriate to give a five-year-old $50 a week.

- If you want to know the going rate for allowances, just ask your children. They are well aware of what their friends get.

- Allowances should have few if any restrictions on them. Most parents encourage saving some of the allowance to teach the child about savings. Naturally, if you do not let your children buy candy, you will probably restrict them using their allowance for candy. However, you should be aware that allowances do encourage freedom.

- Talk to your children about how they spend their allowances. Use the allowance as a way to teach them the value of money.

- When your child gets old enough and responsible enough, you may want to give him or her an additional clothing allowance so that he or she has some control over the clothing bought. This also saves you from those seemingly endless battles over shopping.

- If you give a clothing allowance you will probably feel more comfortable putting some restrictions on it at first. If you absolutely forbid mini-skirts, restrict those. Be prepared for the unhappy child who has spent all his or her money for the month on that one pricey piece of clothing that he or she had to have. Stick by that decision. If you bail the child out and break down and buy him or her the essentials that were neglected, then you have taught your child that he or she does not need to live within a budget.

Earning Money

In addition to allowances, you may want to pay children for extra chores they perform in addition to their regularly assigned duties. Families in which both parents work usually find it necessary to contract out some of the services. For some this means hiring a cleaning lady or sending shirts out to the laundry. If you normally pay someone to mow your lawn, then it would be appropriate to pay your child to mow your lawn. This gives the child additional spending money to save up for those big purchases. Some families post a list of things to be done and the "wages" for doing them, giving their children a chance to make extra money. Other families take bids for extra chores.

Savings

The best way to teach a child about savings is to save money yourself. The standard recommended by most financial planners is that 10 percent of your income should be saved. When your child is young, a piggy bank is adequate. When the child is in elementary school, particularly the upper grades, he or she can be encouraged to open a savings account. A savings account is a good way to teach your child to plan for the future.

Spending Guidelines

Without spending guidelines children will act like many adults. They will spend indiscriminately and wonder where their money went.

- Sit down with your child and have him or her list all of his or her anticipated expenses. If you have told your child that a certain amount must be saved or given to the church, for example, make sure these are included.

- Set a budget with your child. (If you are like many adults and can't stand the term budget, call it something else—capital outlays, expense record or financial plan.)

- Help your child keep track of his or her expenses and compare this with the budget.

- Explain to your child what you have budgeted so he or she has an idea of how you spend your money. Naturally, the amount of detail you go into depends on the child's age and his or her ability to understand. Children who have some understanding of how the family spends its money tend to be more realistic about asking for money.

Working Teenagers, the Tradeoff

Sooner or later your teenager will meet the pressure to work head on. In some families a working teenager is a necessity to pay bills or save for upcoming college expenses. *Statistics show that teenagers who work are better organized and have higher gradepoints.* If your teenager wants to work, discuss with him or her the reason for doing so.

- Will he or she be able to work and maintain the standards you expect ?

- Will he or she be able to take part in activities such as sports, music, drama?

- Will he or she have any social life? This seems to be one of the biggest complaints of the working teenager. From a parent's standpoint, however, this is not all bad!

- Will he or she get enough rest?

The decision to work is a major one and should not be based on "all my friends have jobs," but rather on if it's the right thing for your child.

Modeling Behavior

As with all values, whether it be how to spend money or the use of alcohol, the strongest teacher is your own behavior. If you tell your children they should not drink but you come home drunk, then you are undermining your own teaching. Most of us remember too well a teacher, parent or friend who said, "Do as I say, not as I do." That, of course, is one of the hardest parts of being a parent – living up to your own expectations.

4
COMMUNICATION

Successful parents are ones who communicate with their children and spouses. Once communication breaks down in a family, trouble starts. Unfortunately, many parents feel they are communicating if they tell their children what to do. Although that is a form of communication (giving commands), it is only a small part of the communication process. The three main parts of communication are:

1. **Verbal communication**
2. **Non-verbal communication**
3. **Listening**

If you are aware of only one or two of these three aspects, then you are not fully communicating. This does not mean that your family is in huge trouble, but it does mean that it is liable to have more friction because of misunderstandings.

Verbal Communication

Verbal communication is what most people think of when asked about communication. It is the obvious. You communicate with words either by speaking or writing. But what most people don't realize is that fully *80 percent of what we communicate is nonverbal.* Yes, you read that correctly. Verbal communication is important. Probably the most miscommunication between people takes place verbally when the wrong words are used, particularly inexact words. Comedian Norm Crosby has based his whole career on a routine in which he uses the wrong words. However, in real life the wrong word is not a laughing matter. If you're lucky, your children will "do as you mean, not as you say."

Nonverbal Communication

As previously stated, nonverbal communication is *80 percent of what we communicate.* This includes the tone of voice we use, the way we look when we say something, our body language and even our handwriting. Each of you had experiences with your own parents in which their body language or tone of voice said something very different than the words they used.

If you have a dog, try saying something positive to the dog, such as "Good dog," in the way you would normally scold the dog. He will respond to the tone of voice. With children, the tone of voice is stronger than the words. Have you ever wondered why your children were less than enthusiastic to see you after work? Maybe it's how you greet them or the way you look? Does your body language communicate, "I'm tired, leave me alone"? Do your words say, "Hi, I'm home. How was your day," but your tone of voice says, "I am exhausted. Let me catch my breath"?

Children wonder how parents can tell when they are not telling the truth. Nonverbal communication is the tipoff for Mom and Dad. The subtle clues tell you when something is being left out.

Even written communication can use nonverbal clues. A note written with bold strokes and important words underlined says, "Pay attention. This is important." The same words written in dainty handwriting will not achieve the same effect. Many working parents write notes to communicate instructions. With varying schedules of children and parents, notes are valuable ways of keeping the communication lines open. Not every business place allows personal phone calls, and most schools do not allow children to call except in an emergency. Thus the written note becomes a major way of communicating when schedules do not coincide.

To become aware of and improve your nonverbal communication skills, try to:

• Be aware of how you communicate nonverbally.

- Jot down the actions your children use on a regular basis and what they are attempting to communicate. Does your child grimmace to indicate that he or she is unhappy with what you have said? Does he or she shrug his or her shoulders because he or she doesn't know the answer or is playing dumb?

- Be aware of problems your children may have that are communicated nonverbally. Does your child seem to be lost in his or her own world? Is this part of his or her personality or is he or she worrying about something? If your child starts stuttering or stammering, it could be an indication of a problem. If your child is not normally whiney but starts to be, he or she may be experiencing a problem.

Being aware of nonverbal communication can make you a better communicator. There is a reason, after all, why we say, "Actions speak louder than words."

Listening

Most of us merely hear. We do not listen to what others say. Because we do not listen and are just responding to what is said or are anticipating our next "speech," we make assumptions about what we just heard— assumptions that are faulty because of inadequate information. When you actively listen you:

1. **Focus** on the person and what he or she is communicating. If your child comes home and says, "Several boys and girls got into trouble at school today," is he or she merely reporting or saying that "I was good and you should be proud of me"?

2. **Analyze** what the person is saying. Think about the speaker's verbal and nonverbal communication, and put the conversation into context. If your three-year-old says, "My teddy bear doesn't like the dark," he or she is probably saying, "I don't like the dark and I am scared of it."

3. **Show an interest** in the speaker and what he or she is saying. Your body language must show that you are actively listening. If you turn your back to the speaker, he or she will get the message.

How to Communicate With Your Children

Understanding your children better is one way to better communicate with them. One of the ways you may want to do this is to better understand your child's personality. Every year thousands of people take the Myers-Briggs personality test, a test that classifies personalities into 16 major types. The four areas covered in the test are:

1. Whether the child is an introvert or an extrovert.

2. Whether the child perceives the world primarily through sensory or intuitive perceptions.

3. Whether the child depends primarily on thinking or feelings to make decisions.

4. Whether the child sees time as a continuum or prefers time to be segmented.

Introvert Versus Extrovert

Introverted children are often seen as reserved and contemplative. They prefer to think about what they are going to say and then say it , not wasting any words. Extroverted children, on the other hand, are outgoing and are likely to think while they are talking. They think with their "mouths," eventually formulating the ideas that the introverted children have been quietly thinking about. Introverts prefer private time. In fact, it is absolutely essential that they have time by themselves as they are drained by others, and the private time gives them time to recharge their batteries. Just the opposite, extroverted children live by the credo, "The more the merrier." They are recharged by being with others and are quickly bored with being alone.

Neither type of personality is right or wrong and most children will demonstrate some of each quality. The key is to observe what your child's preferences are. The problem arises when an introverted child is born into a family of extroverts or vice versa. Understanding personality types can help you better communicate with your child. In our family there are two introverts and three extroverts. The two of us who are introverts don't feel at all slighted when the extroverts take off for another of their endless social engagements. We simply retire to our rooms and enjoy the peace. When we all get back together, we're all happily recharged, each in our own way.

- To communicate with introverted children, give them privacy and don't assume that because they aren't playing with other children they are abnormal. Communicate with them on a one-to-one basis or in small groups.

- While the biggest problem in communicating with introverted children is to draw them into conversation; with extroverted children it's being able to get a word in among all their "friends." Conversations "on the run" are the norm.

Sensors Versus Intuitive

Sensor children prefer exact answers, sequential stories and work that has tangible results. They tend to think and perform tasks methodically. They are grounded to the world by their senses. You might say they are no-nonsense children and live in a world of details. Intuitive children, on the other hand, see the big picture, the possibilities. They are concerned about the future. They look for the relatedness of things. They prefer fantasies as stories rather than the "boring" stories about "real things" of the sensor children. Intuitive children can be easily distracted from a task. While sensor children live in a black and white world, intuitive children see the various shades of gray.

- Communicate with sensor children using precise words. They will appreciate your choice. They do not want to know that the party started around 3:00. They want to know it started at exactly 3:12.

- If you are giving them directions, do so sequentially.

- Sensor children are very literal and will be frustrated if you use many word plays and puns.

- If you want sensor children to clean their rooms, tell them exactly what they are to do. "Pick up all your toys and put them in the closet. Make your bed. Put your dirty clothes in the laundry room, etc." The direction, "Clean your room," means little to them.

- To communicate with intuitive children you may give general directions. "Clean your room" will make perfect sense to the intuitive child.

- Intuitive children will love your using word games and puns.

- If you want something done, suggest to intuitive children that they figure out how to do it and how it works. They love understanding how something works.

- Intuitive children do not necessarily need sequential directions and are able to do several things at once.

Thinking Versus Feeling

Thinking children are ones who make decisions based on gathering the facts and then doing what is fair and truthful based on logic rather than feelings. Feeling children make decisions by taking feelings into account. Feeling children tend to be service-oriented and want to please others, while thinking children take pride in being objective. Thinking children also tend to be argumentative. On the other hand, feeling children will seek harmony rather than clarity. (This is the only personality group that tends to be linked to the child's sex. Statistically, boys tend to be thinkers more frequently and girls tend to be feelers.)

- Communicate with thinking children by being logical and presenting the facts. If you set a curfew, explain why in logical arguments.

- Communicate with feeling children by appealing to their emotions. If they are faced with a tough decision, the question to ask them is, "How do you feel about it?"

Perceiving Versus Judging

Many a marriage has fallen apart because one partner was a perceiver and the other a judger. This difference can also cause a strain in a parent-child relationship. The perceiving child is described by some as flighty, always late and an air-head. Actually, that description is too harsh. Perceivers are the ultimate procrastinators. They want to keep all options open and usually wait until the last minute to get things done. They are usually late because they have many other things they attempt to accomplish at once. They tend not to plan, have messy rooms, but are usually spontaneous and creative.

Judging children like to see the world come to closure. They like definite starts and stops. They believe in the saying, "A place for everything and everything in its place." Generally speaking, they don't like surprises, hate to be late and love order in their lives.

- Communication can be frustrating if you are a judger and you have a perceiving child. One of the biggest problems is getting them any place on time. Many parents resort to telling them that something starts 15 minutes before it actually does so the perceiver will arrive "on time."

- However, if you are a perceiving parent, you may be highly frustrated with your judging child. He or she may appear to nag because your life is not in the order that he or she likes. This is particularly true when your child believes that getting to a 1:00 appointment means arriving at 12:45, while to you it means starting for the appointment at 1:00. Sparks may fly.

Four Main Temperaments

Although there are 16 personalities from the results of the Myers-Briggs test, for convenience sake, one can look at four main personalities.

1. NT or the Intuitive(N) Thinker (T)

2. SP or the Sensor (S) Perceiver (P)

3. NF or the Intuitive (N) Feeler(F)

4. SJ or the Sensor (S) Judger (J)

The NT Child

- Lives in a world of ideas.

- Is the thinker.

- Favorite question is "Why?"

- The world seems to pass him or her by.

- Is very serious, seldom plays.

- Has great vision of the future.

- Is found in only one of six children.

- Might be characterized as the scientist or the absent-minded professor.

The SP Child

- Is always on the go.

- Is usually mechanically minded.

- Is concerned with how some hing works rather than why it works.

- Is impulsive.

- Is a spender.

- Is quite often accused of playing more than working.

- Is many times misdiagnosed as hyperactive or attention deficient.

- Is found in one in three children.

- Might be characterized as the "Good Time Charlie."

The NF Child

- Is concerned with finding himself or herself.

- Is looking for the relevance of life.

- Is concerned with meaningful relationships.

- Is very people-oriented.

- Is concerned with words.

- Is only one of every six children.

- Might be characterized as social worker or minister.

The SJ Child

- Is every teacher's dream because he or she understands how the system works and does what he or she is told.

- Is concerned with traditions.

- Is a saver.

- Is a joiner of organizations.

- Is concerned with titles.

- Is the worker and is compelled to work to keep things going.

- Is one of every three children.

- Might be characterized as the pillar of the community.

In a Nutshell

- The NT child asks "Why," and will only do what makes sense.

- The SP child asks "How does it work," and will only do that which is immediately enjoyable.

- The NF child asks "Is it relevant," and will only do that which gives meaning to his or her life.

  The SJ child asks "What is your title," and does what someone in authority says should be done.

Ways to Communicate With Your Children

- Try to be precise. Many communication problems can be eliminated by using exact words. This is particulary important for certain personality types.

- Try to use words they will understand.

- Speak at their level but do not speak down to them. You do not like to be patronized and neither will your children.

- Remember that everyone has worth. Treat your children with dignity and respect.

- Keep your communication simple. There is no need to go into every detail when answering a question. The classic joke of the young boy who wants to know where he came from and receives a full-blown birds-and-bees lecture rather than the answer "Cleveland," is an example of a parent not keeping it simple.

- Communicate on a regular basis. A good relationship between parent and child (and for that matter between husband and wife) is built on regular communication.

- Both good and bad must be communicated, but it is better to be positive than negative. A positive remark seems to hold much more weight than a negative one.

- Remember that your children, like the adults you communicate with, are distinct individuals with their own unique ways of listening, communicating and processing information. Just because they are your children doesn't mean you should communicate effortlessly with them.

Praise, Question and Polish

In teaching writing, the PQP method is a very effective way of getting children to revise their work. You focus on the good (Praise), you challenge what doesn't work (Question), and you suggest ways to revise and make the writing better (Polish). The same method can be effectively used when discussing a problem or disciplining a child.

1. **Praise.** Point out what the child is doing that is good. If the problem is a broken curfew but the child is normally on time, praise the usual behavior.

2. **Question.** Although "why" questions satisfy adults, many times children, particularly small children, have no idea why they did something. Your questions should deal with "how could you have done this differently," or "what were the circumstances behind your action?"

3. **Polish.** The old word here for the traditional family would have been punish. Here though, you are attempting to get the child to change his or her behavior. Punishment may subdue the behavior, but it does not eliminate it. Try to come up with a way to change the behavior. "How can we improve and build on your previous behavior so this problem doesn't appear again," should be the focus.

The PQP method is one way to open up lines of communication because it deals with problems and situations on a positive, constructive basis.

How to Encourage Your Children to Communicate With You

If you make an effort to communicate and actively listen to your children, they will find it easy to communicate with you. You have children, they will find it easy to communicate with you. You have managed the first and most important step: **Keep the communication lines open.** You all know how frustrating it is when the phone goes dead, yet many families operate with an interpersonal "dead-phone" communication system.

Be available. This is hard because two-career parents are usually pressed for time. Some families set aside special times, while others are always aware of the need to be available to communicate with their children.

Listen. Actively listening will encourage your children to communicate with you because it shows you care about what they have to say.

Respond, don't judge. This can be very hard for some parents. If you simply respond with non-judgmental statements such as "I hear you saying...," your child is more likely to share with you his or her concerns. If you judge every statement, your child will soon learn to censor what he or she says to you. This undoubtedly will make for smooth conversation because you won't hear anything unpleasant, but it also means you will probably not know what is going on in your child's life. He or she may then take problems to a willing listener, someone whose values are vastly different than yours.

Find time to be with your children. You alone know what will work out best for your schedule and your children's schedule. If you are going to communicate, you need to find time to be with your children. *There are a variety of ways to do this:*

- Have a routine time when you and your child can talk. For some people this is while doing the dinner dishes, in the car on the way to lessons, or during a family council.

- Choose a time that is conducive to communication. For example, if your teenager is a night owl and a bear in the morning, communicating in the morning is going to be difficult. If it can't wait, try writing it out and letting him or her read it when he or she is awake.

- Set a date with each of your children, once a week for example, when the two of you get together to talk and perhaps do something special like go out to lunch. Thursday mornings are sacred at our house because Mom takes our youngest out for donuts. And since our daughter is an SJ child, it has now become TRADITION. Other parents jog on a regular basis, taking a different child along each time.

No matter what you do, no matter how you choose to spend the time, the bottom line is to keep communication lines open with your children. If you do, you will find parenting an easier experience than it is for most.

5

MEETING YOUR CHILD'S NEEDS

If there's one thing that June Cleaver did well, it was meeting the needs of her children. That perfect role model is one that most of the Baby Boomer generation grew up with and is perhaps the reason why, when coupled with the feminist movement, a new character was introduced into our society: Super Mom. Almost every working mother has been faced with trying to live up to June Cleaver's image and be the ultimate career woman at the same time. It's not possible.

Interestingly, fathers have not been faced with that problem. No one ever uses the term Super Dad. That's probably because society has allowed men to escape the guilt of being both a father and a career man. At our house we have a refrigerator magnet that says, "Why doesn't anyone ever ask a man how he can have a family and a career?"

Meeting your child's needs while working is basically a balancing act. It requires you to:

- Set priorities.

- Divide up responsibilities of parenting.

- Put your family and career in perspective.

- Communicate with your spouse and work together.

If you are an idealist, you will probably have more trouble because you hold high standards for yourself. You do not have to cut back on your standards, but you may need to cut back on the number of items you have standards for. You may be able to only keep a clean house while ignoring the sheets and pillowcases you would like to iron. Choose carefully what you want to be perfect, as you will not have time to do everything perfectly.

Building Self-Esteem

Every parent's goal is to have well-rounded children who are able to cope with the world and eventually make it on their own. However, how does one do this? Each child is different in personality and temperament. At first it may seem impossible, but it is not. Building a child's self-esteem is basically the result of an attitude that the parents have toward the child.

- Treat your children with dignity and respect. Don't ridicule or embarrass them.

- Remember that every child has self-worth. Don't tear away his or her worth by making him or her dependent on you.

- Love your child, even when he or she is being unlovable.

- Give your child a chance for independence at each age.

- Offer positive reinforcement to your child for the good things that he or she does.

This attitude will foster maturity appropriate for the age of your child. One of the hardest things about being a parent is that *you* have to grow up. If you are used to having temper tantrums and continue to do so as a parent, don't be surprised when your child has them also. The best parents are role models for their children.

Self-Esteem Techniques for Different Ages

1. **Infants:** With infants the vast majority of self-esteem building comes from giving them a consistent level of security and love.

2. **Toddlers:** The toddler's world is one of discovery, which can be both exciting and frightening. The self-esteem of toddlers can be undermined if every time they stumble or are scared, you reinforce their fright. This is not to say you should ignore them, but if you are overly responsive, they soon learn that the world is scary and a hurtful place, thus lowering their self-esteem. This is a time when children naturally suffer from separation anxiety. They need to know you are there, but should not be made to feel they can't function without you. It is natural for toddlers to explore the world and start to break away. Set limits that they understand.

3. **Preschoolers:** Once in preschool, building a child's self-esteem becomes the responsibility of the parents and the teacher. If you see your child coming home less confident than he or she previously was, talk to the teacher. The child is going through a new experience (school), so a certain amount of concern by the child is natural. If you have already supplied your child with self-esteem, this momentary lapse is natural. Try to put yourself in your child's shoes. How would you react to the situation?

4. **Elementary-age children:** Your child has now entered a world where his or her self-esteem will be tested daily. Each day the elementary-age child is asked to learn new material, try new ideas, experience new concepts. At this point in your life as a parent you become a coach and cheerleader, encouraging your children, giving them pep talks, showing them that you believe in their abilities. Keeping communication lines open is important at this age.

5. **Preadolescents:** By now school is routine and, although not every child loves school, most have learned the system and how to tolerate it. Self-esteem problems for the preadolescent usually deal with the opposite sex and peer pressure. Once again, the best you can do to help the preadolescent's self-esteem is to keep communication lines open and be an active listener. At this point in your child's life, he or she needs a safe haven for all the emotional and social storms he or she will be going through.

6. **Adolescence:** Just like the kindergartener, the adolescent is faced with a new world when he or she heads out to junior high school or high school. He or she is faced once again with new routines, new situations and increased expectations. To help your adolescent's self-esteem, you need to once again be a coach and cheerleader. During each stage of your child's life, the emphasis on how to help

your child maintain and increase self-esteem may vary. However, your basic attitude toward your child should not. If the child senses that you don't think he or she can do it (whatever it is), then your child will lose self-esteem. Be aware of how you communicate both verbally and nonverbally with your children.

Helping Your Child Grow

Most of you are aware of the various stages of physical growth your children go through. You can't help but be aware because everytime you turn around, they've outgrown their clothes again. But are you aware that your child grows in *five* different ways?

Areas of growth:

1. Physical.
2. Emotional.
3. Mental.
4. Social.
5. Spiritual.

Helping Your Child Grow Physically

You can help your child grow by providing him or her with:

- Healthy, nutritional meals.

- Exercise.

- Rest.

- Routine health checkups.

- Preventative health care.

Helping Your Child Grow Emotionally

The emotional life of your child is interrelated with his or her self-esteem. An emotionally healthy child is a well-balanced child, able to cope with problems, use resources and act independently. You can help your child grow emotionally by:

- Treating your child with dignity and respect.

- Fostering independence.

- Loving your child.

- Helping your child find solutions for problems, not solving his or her problems for him or her.

- Helping your child meet crisis situations in a calm manner.

That's a big order, isn't it? Naturally, it's easier if *you* have matured emotionally.

Helping Your Child Grow Mentally

There are numerous books on the market that tell you how to teach your preschooler and even your infant how to read. Children are being expected to perform at higher levels educationally than ever before. Within the home you can help your child grow mentally by:

- Fostering a spirit of inquiry and curiosity.

- Encouraging reading and writing.

- Encouraging your children to question their universe.

- Providing reference materials in the home so homework can be done efficiently.

- Playing games that expand the mind.

Like self-esteem, mental growth is an attitude, one that doesn't need extensive resources. Every one of us knows a child whose parents pooh-poohed education, but overcame this to become a college professor or other intellectual achiever. For every one of those who have escaped a home that is a mental wasteland, there are 100 such achievers whose parents fostered their mental growth.

Helping Your Child Grow Socially

Our society helps us with this one because many of our social customs and institutions are built around what is socially normal.

- At age 3 Johnny enters preschool.

- At age 5 or 6 Susie enters school.

- At age 8 Mary takes her first communion.

- At age 13 Jacob has his bar mitzvah.

- At age 16 Susie is sweet 16 and never been kissed.

As in other areas of growth, you will be better prepared for what is normal socially with your second child than your first, and with your third child than your second. If you are unsure what your community's standards are, ask around. This does not mean that your daughter has to start dating at age 12 if the majority of her classmates are. But at least you will know what peer pressures you are operating against. To help your child grow socially :

- Encourage appropriate social interaction for your child's age.

- Encourage your child to have friends.

- Be aware of what is socially acceptable for your child's age group in your community.

- Take your child's personality into consideration. Not all children will be ready to socialize at the same time.

- Discuss with your child what is and is not socially acceptable for his or her age.

- Foster independence.

Helping Your Child Grow Spiritually

Many parents are totally unaware or very uncomfortable when it comes to helping their children grow spiritually. A child's spiritual growth is helping the child understand his or her place in the grand scheme of things. For many parents, this means belonging to an organized religion. For others it is showing a deep reverence for life. While for others it is answering the child's questions about life in a matter-of-fact manner. For most children, spiritual awareness is their last area of growth. (Many adults are still growing spiritually.) Most parents will only lay the foundations for spiritual growth.

You can help your child grow spiritually by:

- Answering the "big" questions about life and death, the universe, the meaning of life in a matter-of-fact manner as best you can.

- Encouraging him or her to be active in the organized religion you are active in.

- Encouraging him or her to look at a variety of religions or philosophies if you do not have an organized religion.

- Discussing spiritual matters in your home so that he or she is comfortable with such concepts.

- Agreeing between yourselves, if yours is a religiously mixed family, on the basic concepts you want your child to have.

One of the many rights Americans have is freedom of religion. If you want to bring your child up Catholic, Jewish, Islamic, Atheistic, you may do so. No matter what your religious belief or lack of belief, your child will grow spiritually. He or she will try to understand where he or she fits in this universe. If you do not discuss these issues with your child, someone else will.

Fostering Independence

Throughout this chapter it has been suggested that you foster independence in your children. Two-career parents are in a better position to do this than families in a more traditional setting. Out of necessity, children of two-career families must take on independence because Mom and Dad do not have endless hours to dote on their every need. Fostering independence in a child is important whether both parents are working or not. The child will not be living with you or dependent on you forever. In fact, nature has a way of making adolescence rough enough that we all, both parents and teenagers, breathe a sigh of relief when teenagers decide to move out!

There are a variety of ways to foster independence:

- Encourage your child to do things for himself or herself. If for example, you know that he or she can dress himself or herself, then encourage that. You may be surprised at some of the outfits arrived at, but it gives you an opportunity for teaching your child about color coordination. Have a button made that says, "I dressed myself this morning," thus giving your child pride (and explaining the odd combination when you send him off to preschool).

- Encourage your child to try new things.

- Assign chores that are appropriate for their ages and let them set their own schedules to meet deadlines.

- Don't communicate (verbally or nonverbally) your concern when your child tries out something new. Remember, children are natural risk takers, adults are not. Just because they make one mistake doesn't mean they're washed up for life. This is not to say you should allow your children to do everything they want. As much as a three-year-old wants to play in the street, it is not safe, so you need to set limits. Be realistic, however, in the limits you set. For example, it is unrealistic to tell your children they cannot ride a bike until they are 12 because children are physically and mentally capable of doing so at a much earlier age.

- Give your children opportunities to test their independence in a protective environment.

Appropriate Amounts of Independence

Parents with more than one child have the advantage of knowing what is appropriate in terms of the amount of independence children should have because they have already learned (or experimented) with their first child. Unfortunately, there are not any hard and fast rules about what is appropriate because the amount of independence varies based on individuals, community standards, religious upbringing and cultural standards. For example, observations of friends of ours that live in Sweden show a marked difference between the way independence is viewed for children in Sweden and in the United States. Swedish parents expect their children to be dependent until they start to school at age seven. Then the children are expected to make decisions on their own and act quite independently. American parents are much more gradual in their allowing of independence with 18 being the magic age for complete independence. Some conservative religions allow less social independence than the more liberal religions. The amount of independence you give your child will be based on your religion, community and your personal level of comfort in giving your children independence.

Here are a few (but hardly comprehensive) guidelines:

1. **Infants:** By age one the child can handle being out of sight of a parent or childcare worker for brief periods of time. The infant can still suffer from separation anxiety and will need to check to make sure an adult is around.

2. **Toddler:** By age three, toddlers are capable of dressing themselves (not intricate snaps or buttons), playing away from an adult with minimal supervision (in a safe environment), and walking next door to a friend's house by themselves (in a safe neighborhood, without crossing a street and with parents watching).

3. **Preschooler:** Preschoolers are capable of dressing themselves, selecting their own clothes to wear with minimal supervision, playing unsupervised in a safe environment with an occasional check by an adult, walking to a friend's house nearby, and deciding on what they want to eat in a restaurant with adult limits set on the selection.

4. **Elementary School Age:** School-age children are able to help select their own clothes when purchasing them, walk to school, play unsupervised, decide what they want to eat in a restaurant with adult limits set on price, walk to a friend's house who lives in the neighborhood, do chores on their own schedule (meeting your deadlines), go to an overnight camp, stay overnight at a friend's, go to a movie with a friend without adult supervision (in a safe neighborhood).

5. **The Preadolescent:** The Preadolescents are able to buy their own clothes with guidelines (thus avoiding the more outlandish fads), be given their own money at restaurants and order from the menu on their own, go to the malls with a friend, have their own telephone with guidelines on its use.

6. **The Adolescent:** Adolescents are capable of having their own clothing allowance and living by their "mistakes," driving a car, taking trips by themselves or with friends (the older the adolescent, the longer the trip), having a job and taking on the responsibility that goes with it, choosing their own friends, owning their own car and taking care of it.

Letting Go

How you handle independence as a parent will decide how easily you let go of your children. For many parents, the ages 18 to 22 mark a transitional stage: children going off to college, the service or work, but popping back into your life on vacations, leaves or when they run out of money and need a place to live. If you have encouraged your children to be independent, they will long to be out on their own and the stays at home will become fewer and fewer until finally they will be referred to as visits. Then your child has achieved true adulthood.

You can prepare yourself for letting go by doing so gradually. It has been said that our children are not ours but are merely passing through us. In nature when you nurture something, you give it what it needs to stand on its own. The same is true of children. It is natural to feel both sad and elated when your children finally leave home. And it is natural for them to want to leave home but want to stay. Fostering their independence will help both you and your children make the transition.

Motivation and Rewards

Another way to meet your children's needs is by motivating them and rewarding them for doing something well. Rewards, like discipline and the amount of independence, should be based on the age or maturity of the child. Naturally, what motivates a four-year-old will not motivate a 15-year-old. Even within a particular age group you will find that some children are motivated by material objects while others are motivated by words of praise.

Fair Versus Equal

Do not get caught in the trap that everything must be *equal* among your children. Everything must be *fair*, but fair is not the same as equal. If you treat your children equally then you will have exactly the same standards for each child. Allowing your five-year-old son to date because his 16-year-old brother does is treating them equally. Giving your 16-year-old son the same allowance as his five-year-old brother is treating them equally. However, it is not fair to either child. As much as children do not like to hear it, particularly younger children who want to do what older children are doing, treating them equally is not fair. Strive to find ways to motivate and reward each child based on age and abilities.

Types of Rewards

For some parents, rewards include money or materialistic items. But there are many other kinds of rewards that motivate children.

1. **Physical:** Hugs, kisses, pats on the back, doing something with the child are all types of physical rewards.

2. **Verbal:** "Atta boys" or "Atta girls," praise, "bragging" to others within earshot of your child are types of verbal rewards.

3. **Responsibility:** Giving children more responsibility because they have done a good job will motivate some.

4. **Privileges:** Staying up late, watching television when it's not normally allowed, having a friend overnight, and driving the family car are all possible privileges that may motivate.

5. **Monetary/materialistic:** Paying children, giving them points that may be used to "buy" something, encouraging them to work toward a goal of a new bike or a new outfit are all examples of monetary or materialistic rewards used to motivate.

Plan, Do and Evaluate

There is an old maxim taught in many schools of home economics that says you should *Plan, Do and Evaluate*. If the communication lines are open between you and your spouse, then this is an effective way to meet the needs of your children. Plan on how you are going to meet their needs. What kinds of motivation will you use? How will you foster independence? What can you do to help each of them grow in the five different areas? Then, once you have put your "plan" into action, evaluate its effectiveness as you go along and change it, if necessary, so it is more effective. The fewer rules you use, the easier it is to change.

Remember: *Management is a thinking process.*
As a parent, you are the ultimate manager.

6
DISCIPLINE

Discipline. That word no one wants to talk about. For many of you, discipline means punishment, the type your parents used on you. Discipline is not punishment. Discipline is control and helping your children learn how to control their own behaviors. **The ultimate goal in disciplining is not having to discipline.** In other words, the child becomes self-disciplined. To achieve this you have to show control. This can be difficult when faced with a child that does not behave. Many times the positive benefits of disciplining are diminished if you fly off the handle. If you have just praised a child about how good he or she was because he or she showed so much maturity and then blow up at your neighbor's dog, who is once again in your flower bed, your child will get the message that temper tantrums are okay.

Normal Behavior Problems for Each Age Group

If you've read the chapter on parenting stages, you know that my aunt was a great one for attributing children's problems to the stage they were going through. This is also true for behavior problems. There are some behaviors that show up more at certain ages than others. If your child does not experience these problems during this age, don't fret. Thank the Lord you've been spared.

1. **Ages 0-5:** Learning the meaning of the word "no," biting, hitting, general aggression when having to share or interact with other children.
2. **Ages 5-10:** Fear, lying, sexual play, bad language, baby talk, bed wetting.
3. **Ages 10-13:** Minor rebellion, swearing, snottiness, experimentation with drugs and alcohol, experimentation with smoking, experimentation with sex.
4. **Ages 13-18:** Rebellion, rejection of parental values and lifestyle.

This list makes life as a parent look pretty glum, doesn't it? But the list does not mean your children will experience any or all of these behavior problems. It simply says they might, and it is in the normal range of behavior at that age. Don't be surprised, for example, if you discover your 12-year-old son has tried smoking cigarettes. It does not mean he will smoke the rest of his life. Be concerned, however, if you discover he is smoking a pack a day and has been doing so since he was nine. That is a problem to be dealt with.

Types of Discipline

Unlike June Cleaver who let Ward do the disciplining when he got home, you as a working parent probably do not have clear-cut lines on who is the disciplinarian and who is not. In a two-career family, disciplining is best done by both parents. This means you need to communicate about what is a problem for your children and how to deal with that problem. Your approach should be three-pronged:

1. Keep it simple.
2. Be consistent.
3. Be creative.

Let's take a brief look at each of these.

Keep it simple. If you're like our family (both husband and wife working, sometimes as much as 100 hours a week between us), you don't have time for complicated rules. Our rules tend to be all-encompassing. One of the hard and fast ones at our house is the Golden Rule: Treat others the way you want to be treated. That covers a myriad of situations. Another is: Solve your own problems. This isn't to say that our children can't ask for help (they do), but the rule is extremely useful when they want us to do something they are quite capable of doing themselves. Goal-setting experts point out that a person has difficulty handling more than five goals. This is a good rule of thumb for discipline rules. Make a list of the rules you operate under now and then add any others you think you need. Then simplify that list to five or less. And post it where everyone can see it.

Be consistent. All of you have bosses and most of you would find it very frustrating if your rules at work changed on a regular basis. Children feel the same way. This is not to say you can't change rules, especially ones that are ineffective. But don't change your rules on a whim. If you say that your children are to clean their own rooms, but then tell one of your children he or she doesn't have to, you're not being consistent. Children have a fine sense of what is just. They may or may not point out your lack of consistency, depending on how open your relationship is. But they will harbor feelings of resentment if your inconsistency slights them.

Be creative. As previously stated, management is a thinking process and disciplining a child is a management process. If your four-year-old wants to test you by seeing how loud he or she can yell, the usual type of discipline would be to ask him or her to stop yelling. Then if he or she doesn't do so, make him or her go to her room for not obeying you. The creative discipliner, however, might say, "Since you like to yell so well, I want you to yell and don't stop." At first the four-year-old will think this is fun, but yelling that loudly continuously loses its appeal very quickly, and soon he or she is begging to stop. In both cases, the child has learned that yelling for no good reason is inappropriate.

Physical Punishment

Spanking is one of those topics that no one wants to talk about for fear someone will find out you have spanked your child. In the last 20 years, America's feelings about spanking have made a complete turn around. We have gone from using spanking as a primary tool for disciplining children to if you spank your child the next step is child abuse. Actually, most child-rearing experts admit there are times when spanking is appropriate. The important point is that if you use spanking as a punishment, it should only be done when you are under control. *Spanking a child so you feel better because you are angry is not punishment.* Your child is not your punching bag. Spanking seems to be considered an alternative as a last choice for the child who will not respond to any other type of discipline. It is done after warning, when the parent is under control and always with the parent's open hand on the buttocks. (The old maxim, "This will hurt me more than you," in this case, could be true.) Remember, the first spank is for the child, the rest are only a poor way for parents to vent their anger. Because of current trends, it is understandable why spanking is losing favor with our society.

Time Out

An effective type of discipline for many children is the time out concept. This is used in many elementary schools, and chances are if you haven't tried this before and start now, your child is already conditioned to what happens in a "time out." The concept is simple. You remove the child (thus the time out) from the situation for a period of time, placing them in a neutral spot. You may even want to designate a time out room or chair. The idea is to take them away and give them time to think about what they are doing so they can start to internalize what is right and wrong. Some children even put themselves in time out because they see they have gotten out of hand.

Grounding and Taking Away Privileges

Grounding can be an effective discipline for the older child. For grounding to work, it is best to let the child know the consequences of his or her actions (preventative discipline). The amount of time a child is grounded will vary depending on the infraction and the age of the child. The important things to remember about grounding are:

- Be consistent.
- Be realistic.

Don't ground a child for six weeks because he or she didn't brush his or her teeth. If you do use grounding as a consequence, be prepared to stick by your guns. If you restrict a child to his or her room because he or she watched television an hour longer than allowed and his or her room has a television, then you need to remove the television also. If you use grounding as your only form of discipline, you soon find that your child is always grounded! In other words, think about the consequences of the grounding.

Another discipline often used is taking away privileges, a sort of semi-grounding. If you "ground" your teenager from the car, are you prepared to run them to school, activities and work? In order to effectively restrict privileges, you must be aware of the consequences of the loss of those privileges. As in grounding, the loss of a privilege should be appropriate to the infraction and the age of the child. Too little or too much will be ineffective.

Facing the Music

Another form of discipline that is very effective is making the child "face the music." In other words, if your daughter's softball breaks a neighbor's window, then it is her responsibility to go to the neighbor and apologize and make arrangements to pay for the window. This is very adult behavior and may take your going with her, but she will learn more from having to do this than from being grounded for two weeks. This type of discipline is most effective when the child has done something that affects someone else, thus resulting in a face-to-face confrontation.

Natural Consequences

Natural consequences is a type of discipline that first appeared as a theory about 20 years ago. At the time it was "the" way to discipline children. In actuality, disciplining is like life. You use what is effective for the situation and the child. For many children, natural consequences is quite effective. Let's say, for instance, you have a teenage daughter who is chronically late. The natural consequence of being chronically late is getting left behind. So you do not wait for her. The first time you use this it should be to something she would really like to do. If you take off without her and she doesn't care, then you've introduced a new problem.

If your seven-year-old son can't make it to the dinner table on time because he "has" to watch television, a natural consequence is that his food is cold, he gets only what is left, or he may have to fix himself a sandwich. Our son, when he was young, could never seem to be dressed when we were ready to get him to the babysitter so we could get to work on time. Many a morning was spent with him coming to the car barefooted and shirt unbuttoned until he finally figured out how to get dressed on time. As the fall mornings got colder and colder, the clothes and shoes were on when we were ready to go. Natural consequences. The biggest problems parents have with natural consequences is that they start feeling sorry or guilty for the child thus reinforcing the problem.

Internalizing the Discipline

The ultimate goal as previously stated is to get children to the point that they discipline themselves. This will be accomplished if you:

- Are consistent in your discipline.

- Are realistic in your expectations.

- Let the child take the responsibility for his or her own discipline.

- Discipline in love not anger.

- Foster independence in the child.

Setting Limits

Setting limits is a fact of life. And by setting limits for your children, you are in a sense preparing them for life. Every year hundreds of laws are passed with the hope that they are for the good of everyone. These are limits that adults have to live with. In your career, it is highly unlikely you are allowed complete freedom. Your company sets limits on what you can and cannot do, so it is natural that a child has limits, also. As a child grows older and learns to discipline himself or herself, he or she will start to come up with his or her own limits. Many teenagers do not have curfews because they are capable of setting their own limits. And many parents' attitude is, "If you can show me you are mature, you can have more say in your limits." For the younger child, limits are a necessity because we as parents are "wiser and more experienced." Limits give life a structure, a framework.

Deciding Limits

The limits placed on a family should be decided by both parents if possible. If you have a family council, discussing the limits with the children is a good idea. Quite often children are actually stricter than the parents. In deciding the rules:

- Keep it simple.
- Be consistent.

If you are willing to take the risk, an effective way of setting limits is to sit down with your child and discuss what the limits will affect, what those limits will be, and the consequences of breaking the limits. This gives the child some ownership in his or her life. *This does not work in a parent-dominated family such as the Dictator Family or the Benevolent Dictator Family.*

Creating Appropriate Expectations

All of us tend to start out with grand plans and expectations for our children. The song "My Boy Bill" in the musical *Carousel* explores the expectant father's dreams about his future child, all very grandiose. The older you get and the more children you have, the more realistic your plans and expectations become. This is not to say that grand plans are wrong, but most goal-setting experts agree that goals should be attainable, otherwise they are merely dreams.

To create appropriate expectations you should:

1. **Be realistic.** If your child has no musical ability, don't expect him or her to become a musician. If your teenager is always late by 20 minutes, move his or her curfew up a half an hour so that he or she will be home on time when you expect him or her to be. Teach your children that life isn't fair. The best way to deal with it is by being optimistic and by laughing. Ask yourself, "Who would you rather be around, someone who is laughing or someone who is down in the dumps?" Children need to see the world realistically. They need to see that they don't always get what they want just because they want it. The optimist and the pessimist may end up at exactly the same ending point in life, but the optimist will have had a good time getting there.

2. **Practice moderation.** Many of the great philosophies of the world strive for a balance. Extremes in the life of a two-career family only add difficulties. Set moderate, attainable goals for yourself and your children. You can always increase them later. Is it realistic to expect each of your children to take piano lessons, be involved in a sport after school, take dance lessons and be involved in Scouts? For Super Mom this is realistic if she has Super Kids, but for working parents this is an unrealistic expectation for you and your children.

3. **Be resourceful.** Tap into the talents you and your family have. The saying, "When life gives you lemons, make lemonade," is being resourceful. If you base your expectations on reality and are resourceful about what you and your family can do and achieve, you should have few problems.

Conflict Management

The object of any conflict management is to get the two parties to calmly look at the problem and negotiate a solution. Sounds great doesn't it? But on a day-to-day basis, being the Grand Adjudicator is *tiring!* Here are some possible solutions to conflict management in a family.

- If you use The Family Council model, use it to settle disputes.

- Assign a time when you or your spouse will "listen" to the arguments. (Most, by the way, will be forgotten—settled out of court—before they ever get to you.)

- Establish the rule that all arguments and replies must be written out.

- Act as a negotiator between the parties who are fighting.

- Make an arbitrary but equal decision. When our children fought over a favorite chair to sit in while watching television, we assigned seats that rotated on a weekly basis. Everyone got a chance to sit in the chair and the fighting stopped.

- Teach your children to identify the reason for the argument.

- Teach your children to attack the issue, not the person. For example, if they are fighting over what television show to watch, the issue is the show. They should not call each other names and should refrain from straying into other unresolved issues. Here is where you will have to be a referee.

- If possible, negotiate behavior to prevent fights. For example, you might say to your children, "When Bobby and Jen arrive today to play, they will probably want to play with your new toys. What are you going to do when they ask?" This anticipates the problem and defuses it.

- If your child encounters a bully, listen carefully to what he says about the situation so you are fully informed about what has happened. Some children seem to gravitate toward the bully types because they see themselves as victims. If you think this is the case for your child, contact the school counselor or your family doctor for advice and possibly psychiatric counseling. If, however, you feel this is just a case of a bully picking on whomever is handy, contact the school authorities and the bully's parents.

Handling the "Difficult" Child

Difficult depends on who you are talking to. We know of one family who had two children of their own and then adopted four more children, one who is deaf and one who is mentally retarded. Both parents work outside the home. To most parents that is a difficult situation because they couldn't cope with it. But this family copes quite well. What you may define as a difficult child may for the next person seem perfectly normal. There are a few situations that would try the patience of most parents:

1. **Aggression in younger children:** This usually takes the form of hitting, biting and kicking for the toddler through kindergartener. First, control the behavior when it happens in the way you would normally discipline the child. If time out works for you, then use it. Swift action for the toddler is better than "explaining" to him or her what is wrong. Then identify, if you can, why the child is resorting to this kind of behavior. Aggressive behavior usually indicates the child is under some kind of emotional stress. It is not uncommon, however, for the child to go through a phase of aggressive behavior. This can be treated with normal discipline. Aggressive behavior because of emotional stress may be handled by alleviating the stress. For example, if your child starts hitting to get attention because he or she is jealous of his or her new baby sister, you can easily make an effort to give him or her more attention. If you find you can't alleviate the stress, seek professional help.

2. **Lying and stealing:** The root of lying and stealing for the school-age child is the same as aggression in the younger child and can be treated in the same way.

3. **Drug and alcohol abuse:** If you suspect that your child is using and abusing drugs and/or alcohol, don't be surprised if when confronted, he or she denies it. Most of us are not equipped to handle drug or alcohol abuse without some support system.

You can get help from:

- family and friends

- hotlines and referral services

- alcohol treatment programs

- employee assistance programs

- mental health agencies

- alcoholism and drug abuse counselors

- your physician or other health professionals

- your child's school counselor

  Check the Yellow Pages under "Alcoholism" for organizations in your area. Don't try to deal with the problem alone.

4. **Antisocial:** The first thing you must decide is whether your child is indeed antisocial. If the child is introverted and you are extroverted, what may seem antisocial to you may be normal for the child. If you are concerned, discuss the child's "antisocial" behavior with his or her counselor and ask for suggestions on how to improve his or her behavior.

5. **Learning disabled:** There are many different learning disabilities. In fact, most of us have something that has hampered our ability to learn. However, we have learned to compensate. The learning disabled child is one who is of average or above average intelligence, but has some serious problems in acquiring knowledge. These can range from dyslexia (difficulty in learning to read) to dysgraphia (difficulty in reading numbers) to attention deficit disorder (short attention span, impulsive, immature for his or her age) among others. If you suspect that your child is having difficulty learning, contact his or her teacher for help. Learning disabled children *are* capable of learning. They just need to be taught in different ways than most children, and they certainly can be successful. Some learning disabled adults that you may know are Tom Cruise, Nelson Rockefeller and Einstein.

  In all cases, the "difficult" child needs more attention and understanding. The best a parent of a "difficult" child can do is to become knowledgeable about the "difficulty" and seek professional help.

Sibling Rivalry

  Sibling rivalry is normal and will not go away. *You can minimize it by working on communication skills in the family and by working on conflict management.* These two areas will reduce the amount of sibling rivalry. One of the things that is helpful in understanding sibling rivalry, besides understanding the dynamics between different children's personalities, is understanding birth order. Most families today have only two children, so we'll look at how birth order affects families of two or three children.

The first born or only child: (A child is considered an only child if there are five years or more between him or her and the next sibling.) The first born child tends to be the child you can rely on. He or she is a perfectionist, and because parents usually have high expectations for their first born, he or she tends to be serious and scholarly. He or she has to carry the banner for the family. On occasion he or she becomes an underachiever because he or she cannot live up to his or her family's ideals.

The second born: The second child must find a niche for himself or herself so he or she tends to take on characteristics opposite of the first child. He or she tends to be the mediator in the family, the peacemaker. He or she doesn't like conflict. While the oldest looks for guidance from his or her parents, the second born has extreme loyalty to his or her peers. He or she is seen by many as a maverick and independent.

The third born: The third child is a people person. He or she too has had to carve out his or her own niche in the family. He or she is usually charming, a salesperson. He or she is also manipulative, having learned the "ways of the world" from his or her older siblings. Since he or she is the "baby" of the family, he or she is quite often treated as the baby, a term he or she generally hates. He or she learns that showing off and blaming others are tolerated because he or she is the youngest.

Naturally, all of these different personalities, brought on by where the child was born in the family, are potential rivalries.

Coping with sibling rivalry is only one of many situations in which you will find yourself disciplining your children. Remember, the ultimate goal in disciplining is to not have to discipline—to have the child become self-disciplined. If you discipline in a consistent manner and make your children take responsibility for their actions, you are on the road to not having to discipline.

7

ORGANIZE, DON'T AGONIZE

If there is one universal problem faced by two-career families it is having enough time to get everything done. In the 1950's sitcoms, being a housewife was a full-time job. Today it is still a full-time job on top of a career. If you don't believe that, ask any working woman whose husband does not help. If you are going to have two careers in your family, everyone has to help at home. Two-career dads and children cannot expect the "luxuries" of a second income without some of the sacrifices. How you as a couple and a family decide to divide up those responsibilities is up to you. Be creative. There is nothing that says certain jobs are gender-oriented. If Dad is a better cook, let him cook. And if Mom likes to mow the lawn, let her. Part of the excitement today is that we don't have to be stuck with Ward and June Cleaver's role models. We have choices and can make our family uniquely ours.

Setting Priorities

It is essential that you and your spouse (and your children if you are using a Family Council) set some priorities. As previously stated, "Management is a thinking process." Perhaps the wife and husband of the 1950's could get along without extensive planning. But busy people have to plan, and a plan works best if you have priorities. Make a list of all the things you and your family want to accomplish in the next year. Ask your children for their input. You may be surprised that they have some of the same goals you have. Participating will give them some ownership of the family's priorities. Rank these goals as a family. Decide on the top three to five, then post them where everyone can see them. For example, your goals might be for everyone to become more physically fit, have a cleaner house and watch less television. From that list, plan how you can accomplish your goals. Sounds like exercising while vacuuming or dusting is a possibility!

You may also want to set priorities for spending your money, deciding which rules the family should have, how your free time will be used, and so on. If you have a plan, even the sketchiest one, you will not feel that life is passing you by. You have the choice. You can control life or it can control you.

Finding Time

We are all given the same amount of time—24 hours a day. But some people seem to have more time than others. Other people can't seem to find time to get anything done. I suspect they're spending their time searching for time. Those that have time, make time. People ask my wife and I how we have time to read when we are both working long hours. First of all, it's a priority for us. Secondly, we make time to read. We don't watch much television, for example, or we let the dustballs grow. All of us have known people who are incredibly busy but who made time for a hobby, built their own home or did volunteer work. These are people who have learned to set priorities and make time for those things they see as important. They have learned to control their time.

Cutting Corners

No one ever died from a dustball. The way your family cuts corners may not be the same as the way the next family cuts corners, but balancing two careers and a family does require cutting corners. One of the corners many people cut is the amount of housework they do. For some, spring cleaning means sorting belongings for a garage sale, and, although the house is not as thoroughly clean as it could be, at least you've made some money off of your "junk." Others cut corners by buying services and more leisure time. Paying someone to clean your house was unthinkable in the 1950's, but it is seen today as one of those added "luxuries" that comes with two incomes. Some people choose to eat out or rely on convenience foods as a way to cut corners. The important thing is that the choice is up to you.

Setting Up Routines

Establish routines for your family so everyone knows what to expect at any given time. Although some people see routines as the "rat race," most of us would find it very difficult to work in a business where there were no routines or procedures. Businesses have over the centuries realized that routines and procedures mean more efficient production. A family will function better (and be more productive) if it, too, has routines to follow.

- Base your routines on your priorities.

- Schedule your routines and post the schedule.

- Make up a master calendar and post it. Insist that your family place their appointments, events and deadlines on the master calendar so there are no surprises.

Preventative Planning

There's an old saying, "A stitch in time saves nine." It's a thought that should be tatooed on the arm of every working parent who's ever met themselves coming and going. Preventative planning is planning so that you don't have to spend all of your time doing things at the last minute or making extra trips that waste time. For example, some families shop at the grocery store every day. That's fine if it's a priority, but it isn't necessarily efficient. With preventative planning you would make menus for the week and shop once a week. Sound boring? Probably. The point, though, is efficiency, not excitement. The possibilities are endless with a little creative thinking.

- Buy your Christmas presents all throughout the year to take advantage of the bargains, to avoid the holiday rush.

- Make Christmas gifts follow a theme and order all of your gifts at the same time. For example, this year everyone gets a magazine subscription, or this is the year of the t-shirt, etc.

- Have gifts wrapped at the store unless, of course, you love to wrap gifts. And if possible have them delivered.

- Wrap one or two boxes at Christmas each year with special paper and a lid that is wrapped so it can easily be removed. Save the boxes and use them again and again.

- Order your clothes from catalogs rather than spending endless hours shopping. This won't work, of course, if you see shopping as a form of recreation.

- To save time shopping, establish rapport with one or two sales people at shops you like, and have them call you when items you need come in or when there are sales.

- Have your colors done so you only buy clothes that are flattering to you. When you adopt a basic color scheme everything will mix and match. This is true for both men and women.

- The simpler the hairstyle, the less time it takes.

- Color coordinate your children so they have no trouble "pulling from their drawers" and looking fine. Johnny always wears red, white and blue. Sally always wears yellow, green and blue. Work around a major triad on the color wheel.

- Buy a packaged trip for your vacation where all the decisions are made for you. My uncle (who has five children) always said, "Are you taking a vacation or are you taking the kids?" Make your vacation relaxing. Seek out vacations that cater to families and that entertain your kids during the day (dude ranches, snow skiing, etc.).

- Plan family gatherings well in advance so "touchy" relatives who don't understand your lifestyle have time to think about why you can't spend every holiday with them.

- Try to schedule all of your children's lessons on the same day so you keep "chauffering" to a minimum.

- Plan one activity a week involving everyone in the family. Too often without planning, families seem to pass each other in the dark. Our family eats Sunday dinner with friends at a restaurant every Sunday. We all look forward to it, and surprisingly quite a few important family issues are discussed. With "observers" there's less of a tendency to argue!

Keep It Simple

If you've been reading this handbook, you've seen this thought several times. You simply do not have time to do too many complicated things. Don't eliminate those things that are important to you, but do try to simplify your life. Many of these are found in the next section on timesavers. For example, we know a lady who for years has "killed" herself at Christmas baking a dozen different cookies. Last year she decided to make only one kind, her family's favorite, and no one complained. She said she actually enjoyed the Christmas season for a change. She made a few extra and got in on a cookie exchange, thus getting a variety of cookies. Other ways to cut corners and gain free time include:

- Mowing take too much time? Put part of your yard into groundcover.

- Plan all of your birthday celebrations to land on the family time. If the government can move the holidays to Mondays, you can celebrate birthdays during your family times rather than on the actual birthdate.

- Send Christmas cards only to those people out of town. Better yet, call them.

- Don't cook gourmet meals unless that is a hobby for you.

- Get an answering machine to save you from having to answer the phone all the time.

Be creative, but simplify! Just because your mother did it doesn't mean you have to.

Timesavers

Most of the ideas already suggested are also timesavers because when you simplify, set priorities and plan you are saving time. With the risk of sounding like "Here's Heloise," here are a few others.

- Make lists and use them.

- Don't waste time waiting. Do something. Carry a book with you, balance your checkbook, write a letter, make a list of things to do tomorrow.

- Buy services. Remember time is money. If you want to take the time, fine, but it may be better, for example, to pay someone to mow the lawn, clean your house, address your Christmas cards.

- Set priorities on your time.

- Eat out, buy convenience foods or prepare and freeze meals in advance (a microwave can be a great timesaver).

- Plan menus and stick to them.

- Divide up responsibilities, giving family chores to those who enjoy doing them whenever possible.

- Clean for company, straighten for sanity.

- Use a standard list when grocery shopping. Most people buy the same things each week, so standardize your list.

- Never serve a gourmet meal, even for company, unless you enjoy doing so.

- Entertain casually, unless you enjoy doing otherwise.

- Teach everyone in the family how to run all the basic appliances and prepare the basic meals.

- Throw out the television. It demands too much time. If that's not realistic, put restrictions on when or how much the television can be watched.

- Buy duvets (covers for down or synthetic-filled comforters) for your beds. The comforter or blankets fit in between two sheets sewn together like a huge pillow case. Making the bed is a matter of pulling over one duvet. Popular in Europe and smart for busy families.

- Have each person in the family do his or her own laundry on an assigned day. One time of pink undershorts will be all it takes before "I'm-too-dumb-to-figure-this-laundry-stuff-out" will become smart. (The washer and dryer are not any more complicated to use than the VCR!)

- Don't iron. If it has to be ironed, it's the responsibility of the person who picked it out.

- Wash all clothes in the washing machine. If your machine has a delicate cycle and a cold wash/cold rinse cycle, even your hand washing can be washed in the machine. Believe me. We've been doing it for years.

- Hang up clothes immediately from the dryer so they don't wrinkle. If you forget to do that, throw in a wet item and dry for a few more minutes, then hang them up.

- Run your car through the car wash that is free with a fill. Don't waste your time washing your own car unless it's your hobby.

- Put big wastebaskets in every room. They take longer to fill and don't have to be emptied as often.

- Use your commuting time to organize your day (if you ride instead of drive). If you drive, listen to tapes that improve your mind. For example, learn that language you've been wanting to. Listen to a world-renowned actor read one of the books on tape you've wanted to read but didn't have time to.

- Keep your meals simple. If it has more than three main ingredients, three preparation steps, and takes more than 30 minutes to prepare, it's time-consuming.

- Use the summer as an excuse to use discretionary china as a friend of ours calls paper plates.

- Organize your children's chest of drawers by clothes color to help them put away their own clothes. All the white clothes in the top drawer, blue in the second, and so forth. It isn't the logical way (underwear, jeans, shirts, etc.), but it makes sense to kids.

- If you can't live without pets, appoint a zookeeper. Even the littlest member of the family can feed the dog or cat.

Message Center

You may have grown up in a small town or rural area before dial phones were introduced. "Central" was the town message center. He or she would relay messages from neighbor to neighbor and even within families. "Central, when my kids get home at 3:00, would you ring them up and tell 'em I'm over at Maudie's?" Today "Central" has been replaced by the refrigerator. It is the place where American messages are left. Establish a place in your home to leave messages and encourage each of your children and your spouse to leave all messages there. If your children are too young to write understandable messages, use an inexpensive tape recorder to leave messages on. This can be effective for phone messages because they can turn on the tape recorder and record the message.

Structure and Routines

While the values you instill in your family are the foundation, the structure is what makes the family operate as a unit. A home without some sort of structure is a chaotic one with no one in charge and everyone working against each other. This is not to say you have to run your home like a Navy admiral. You need the human touch to impose some structure.

One way to do this is to assign family work. Notice I said *family* work. Every family member contributes so the family can function. In the Cleaver family, June took care of the house, Ward brought in the money, and Wally and the Beaver brushed their teeth and washed behind their ears. Life was so simple then. Now, for the two-career family to function, each person must pitch in and help, from the youngest to oldest.

Assign work according to ability and age. A three-year-old boy can set the table, for example, and pick up his toys while his 16-year-brother can cook supper and clean his room.

Two theories of how work should be assigned:

1. *Each person has a chance over a period of time to do each task.* Each person in the family takes turns doing the various tasks set out by the parents or family council. For one week, for example, you cook; the next week clean up the kitchen; the next week vacuum; etc. The theory is that everyone ought to learn how to do all kinds of work. The reality is that it will probably be harder to get some of the work done. If the work isn't done, peer pressure will be the first motivator to get it done because other members of the family will "remind" the non-worker that he or she isn't doing his or her part. Some families set up consequences for the person who doesn't do his or her work.

2. *Assign work based on who wants to do the work.* The theory here is that you have family members doing jobs they enjoy and are good at. The reality is that there may easily be more volunteers for one job than you need and none for another. At our house we always have two that want to clean the bathroom but not do dishes. The solution to this problem is to rotate those jobs that are in high demand.

Clearly state who the boss is. Every job site needs a foreman. Sometimes parents play so many roles they forget which parent is the boss in a particular situation. Ward and June had it easy. Ward was the boss. Since parents in two-career families play multiple roles, decide before the work is assigned who will supervise and evaluate the finished product.

Coping With Stress

With two careers and children, stress is inevitable but it does not have to be destructive. If you plan, set priorities, keep it simple, and keep communication lines open, you can avoid and defuse stress.

Stress signs: Each person reacts differently to stress. The following are some of the ways stress may manifest itself.

- *Unusual fatigue.* This can be a signal for serious illnesses so it should not be treated lightly.

- *Crankiness.* If you are snapping more and more at your children or spouse, you may be under stress.

- *Increased incidents of illness.* This is your body's way of slowing you down.

- *Forgetfulness.* Some people are just naturally absent-minded. But if you aren't normally, you may be experiencing stress.

- *Stomach pains.* For some this is a pre-ulcer condition.

- *Mild depression.*

- *Slight panic.*

- *Back pain.*

- *Tension headaches.* These are usually in the back of the neck.

Do not confuse these with sinus headaches, migraines or cluster headaches. Tension headaches are brought on by tensing of muscles.

Identifying the Reason for Stress

The first step in eliminating or reducing stress is to analyze what causes the stress. For most of you this is fairly easy. Job, family, money or the lack of it are all familiar stress producers. *You can identify the source of your stress by:*

- Making a list of all the things that are worrying you.

- Deciding on a plan of action. Taking action will alleviate some of the stress.

- After you have started the plan, evaluate its effectiveness.

People tend to meet problems and crises in one of three ways.

1. Freeze

2. Fight

3. Flee

Stress is best eliminated by fighting, by identifying it, figuring out a strategy to combat it, and then taking action. When you freeze, the stress doesn't go away, and fleeing is usually impossible to do.

Helping Children Cope With Stress

It would be nice to think that children don't experience stress, and it is true that most children probably lead fairly stress-free lives. But on occasion your child may be under stress. The signs of stress are similar to adult symptoms:

- Bedwetting.

- Thumbsucking if the child has previously stopped.

- Crying, especially in situations when he or she would normally not cry.

- Aggressive behavior such as hitting, kicking and biting.

- Nightmares.

- Withdrawal, antisocial behavior.

- Reluctance to do what he or she would normally do.

- Belligerence.

- Bullying.

You can help a child cope with stress by first identifying the cause. If the communication lines are open, this may be fairly easy. If you ask your child if anything is bothering him or her, you are not likely to get an answer. You need to phrase your questions so they don't sound like you are prying. For example, if you suspect it's a new teacher that is causing the stress, you might say, "I hear Mr. White can be pretty strict. Is that true?" If the child says, "Yes," then proceed with questions to find out if the strictness of the teacher is the problem.

Once you have identified the stress producer, you will need to do the same as you would for yourself. However, you will need to be actively involved in deciding the plan. The child may not be emotionally capable of handling a solution without help.

External Coping Devices

Some people yell, some slam doors, and some kick the dog, at least in the comics. All of these are ways of externally coping with stress. Anything that relieves some of the physical tension of stress is an external coping device. For many people, the most popular outlet is exercise. Exercise as a stress reliever is well-documented and works equally well for children and adults. There's nothing like a brisk walk around the block to clear your head (and your dog will love it, too).

Meditation/Relaxation

Another way of reducing stress is to meditate or learn a relaxation technique. There are many different types of meditation from transcendental meditation to prayer that can help a person cope. Each in its own way does help because it causes people to focus on themselves and clear their minds of extraneous thoughts. Relaxation works on the principle that you teach your body to methodically relax through a set of exercises. Many different meditation and relaxation techniques are widely available.

Priorities

One fairly easy way to reduce stress is to set priorities. Quite often stress is produced because you try to do too many things at once which, of course, is physically impossible. By setting priorities and deadlines you are consciously deciding what will be done and what will not be done, thus eliminating some of the stress-producing guilt. Once you have your priorities set, then you are ready to form a plan and get down to business.

Support Systems to Deal With Stress

If communication is good in your family, then you probably already have a support system set up to help you cope with stress. Support systems are simply people to talk to when you are feeling stressed. They can be friends, spouses, co-workers, and, in an institutionalized form, a telephone number to call for help with a caring but objective person on the other end of the phone. In the days of small-town America and before the advent of television, the backyard fence or the front porch became the meeting places of many a neighbor and served as a way to relieve stress by talking about problems. With change came more mobile lifestyles and the loss of that human touch. For some, support comes from the coffee klatch at work, the bowling league on Tuesday nights, the church choir, the Mothers for Better Schools committee, or other community or religious groups.

Setting Up Support Systems

Another area that is vital to the two-career family is a support system to help deal with crises and childcare. Before two-career families, filling out a school emergency card on who to call was hardly necessary. Everyone knew that Mom was home. Today it is absolutely essential that you and your spouse have a well-thought-out emergency plan.

Daily Support Systems

A daily support system is simply who you rely on when your normal babysitter is unable to work. If you are using daycare, this is not a problem because there will be adequate care if one of the workers is sick. If you use a babysitter and he or she becomes sick, you need to have an alternative plan. Do you have a relative or friend that can pinch hit? Does your company have an emergency-leave policy that covers such a day? Can some sort of dual care be worked out between you and your spouse with each of you taking off part of a day?

You will also need to have a plan for support during a crisis. Crisis support is when your child is sick for an extended period of time, longer than you and your spouse can cover through leaves your jobs may allow. Some cities have programs at the hospital for the child that is not seriously ill, such as with a cold, to come to the hospital as a daycare center until he or she is ready to go back to his or her regular childcare. Once again you need to explore the possibilities of a relative, friend, hiring a nurse, or hospital daycare as a way to cope with a sick child that cannot go to regular childcare.

You also need to have a plan to deal with the illness of your school-age child who normally would be in school. Some children are capable of staying home by themselves armed with emergency numbers, a handy telephone, a television and chicken soup. Others will need some sort of in-home care.

Childcare

For the working couple, childcare can be one of the biggest concerns and a never ending struggle. Your choices are:

- Daycare center.

- Babysitter outside your home.

- Babysitter in your home.

- Daycare at your place of business.

- Relative or friend who babysits for free.

- Relative or friend who babysits for room and board.

- Nanny.

- You and your spouse working opposite shifts or working out a flex-time situation so one of you cares for the child while the other works.

- Working at home.

Some options may not be realistic because of your circumstances. It is not feasible, for example, for two teachers to work out of their home, work opposite shifts, or probably afford a nanny. Many of you do not have a relative or friend willing to babysit either for free or for room and board.

Once you have limited your choices you then need to evaluate the childcare available. Some of the items you should look at are:

- Are the childcare workers or the babysitters qualified?

- Is the childcare facility or the babysitter licensed?

- What is the caregiver/child ratio? Does it conform to state or national guidelines for the age of your child?

- Will the childcare meet your needs in terms of schedule?

- Is the cost of the childcare within your budget?

- Is the childcare easily accessible?

- Does the childcare have plans for emergencies such as a fire, tornado, earthquake, etc.?

- Would you, if you were a child, like to spend your day in this childcare situation?

- What is the policy concerning the child's lunch, snacks, nap?

- Does the caregiver have adequate indoor and outdoor play equipment?

- What is the policy concerning children with illnesses?

- Does the caregiver have some sort of learning program?

- How are misbehaving children disciplined?

- Is the childcare facility clean and cheerful?

- What is your gut feeling about the childcare?

Once you have chosen a daycare arrangement, it doesn't hurt to drop by unexpectedly to assess the environment, how the children are being handled, etc.

Community Resources

An area often overlooked by parents when they are dealing with support systems is community resources. One previously mentioned is the hospital that offers daycare for the sick child. Many nursing schools will provide names of babysitters (evening rather than full time). Church groups such as a young couples group or a working parents group provide support for working parents. Many hospitals and libraries have tape banks available that can be called for quick information about a particular illness or situation. Community centers sometimes offer programs for the working parent complete with babysitting. For parents who are stressed out and feel they might abuse their children, there are hotlines available to call. Calling "Information and Referral" can give you valuable resources for help. To complete your support system, explore community resources as a viable alternative.

Summary

This is an exciting time to parent because your options are greater than ever before. You have a chance to forge your own unique family, but the excitement is tempered by decisions. Never before have parents been so in control of their families. The role models you grew up with are gone or disappearing. The traditional family (Mom at home, Dad at work, and the kids in the backyard swinging on the picket fence) now comprise less than 20 percent of all families. Thirty-three percent of all families are single-parent families. Step-families are a reality many of you live with, and the sandwich family (grandparents living with their children and grandchildren) are becoming more prevalent.

So the choice is up to you. Good luck!

INDEX

RESOURCE GUIDEBOOKS

Albert, Linda. *Linda Albert's Advice for Coping With Kids.*
E.P. Dutton, Inc.: New York, 1982.

Ames, Louise, Frances L. Ilg and Sidney M. Baker. *Your Ten-to-Fourteen-Year Old.* Delacorte Press: New York, 1988.

Balter, Lawrence. *Who's in Control? Dr. Balter's Guide to Discipline Without Combat.* Poseidon Press: New York, 1988.

Bettleheim, Brunno. *A Good Enough Parent.* Alfred A. Knopf: New York, 1978.

Brazelton, Dr. T. Berry. *On Becoming a Family.* Dell Publishing Co.: New York, 1982.

Brazelton, Dr. T. Berry. *Infants and Mothers.* Delacorte Press: New York, 1983.

Brazelton, Dr. T. Berry. *Toddler and Parents.* Dell Publishing Co.: New York, 1972.

Brazelton, Dr. T. Berry. *To Listen to a Child*. Addison-Wesley:
Reading, Massachusetts, 1984.

Calladine, Carole and Andrew Calladine. *Raising Siblings*.
Delacorte Press: New York, 1979.

Christophersen, Edward. *Little People, Guidelines for Common
Sense Child Rearing*. Overland Press: Shawnee Mission,
Kansas, 1977.

Dinkmeyer, Don and Gary D. McKay. *The Parent's Guide:
Systematic Training for Effective Parenting of Teens*.
American Guidance Service: Circle Pines, Minnesota, 1983.

Dodson, Dr. Fitzhugh. *How to Discipline With Love*.
New American Library: New York, 1978.

Dobson, Dr. James. *Parenting Isn't for Cowards*. World Books:
Waco, Texas, 1987.

Dobson, Dr. James. *The Strong Willed Child: Birth Through
Adolescence*. Tyndale House Publisher: Wheaton, Illinois, 1978.

Dyer, Dr. Wayne W. *What Do You Really Want for Your Children?*
William Morrow and Co., Inc.: New York, 1985.

Eyre, Linda and Richard Eyre. *Teaching Children Responsibility*.
Ballentine Books: New York, 1982.

Faber, Adele and Elaine Mazlish. *How to Talk so Kids Will Listen
and Listen so Kids Will Talk*. Avon: New York, 1982.

Faber, Adele and Elaine Mazlish. *Liberated Parents, Liberated
Children*. Avon: New York, 1975.

Faber, Adele and Elaine Mazlish. *Siblings Without Rivalry*.
Nightingale-Conant: Chicago, 1988.

Ferber, Dr. Richard. *Solve Your Child's Sleep Problems*.
Simon & Schuster: New York, 1985.

Field, David. *Family Personalities*. Harvest House Publishers:
Eugene, Oregon, 1988.

Gordon, Dr. Thomas. *Parent Effectiveness Training: The Tested New Way to Raise Responsible Children.* Peter H. Wyden, Inc.: New York, 1970.

Kiersey, David and Marilyn Bates. *Please Understand Me: Character and Temperament Types.* Prometheus Nemesis Book Company: Del Mar, California, 1984.

Leach, Penelope. *Your Baby and Child.* Knopf: New York, 1978.

Leman, Kevin. *The Birth Order Book.* Dell Publishing Co.: New York, 1987.

Olds, Sally Wendkos. *The Working Parents Survival Guide.* Bantam Books: New York, 1983.

Rubenstein, Dr. Mark. *The Growing years: A Guide to Your Child's Development From Birth to Adolescence.* Atheneum: New York, 1988.

Samuels, Dr. Mike and Nancy Samuels. *The Well Baby Book.* Summit Books: New York, 1979.

Samuels, Dr. Mike and Nancy Samuels. *The Well Child Book.* Summit Books: New York, 1982.

Turecki, Dr. Stanley. *The Difficult Child.* Bantam Books: New York, 1987.

White, Burton L. *The First Three Years of Life.* Prentice Hall: New York, 1975.

Appendix B
RESOURCE PHONE NUMBERS

Active Parenting
Atlanta, GA: 800-235-7755

Agency Information and Referral Service,
24-Hour Confidential Crisis Intervention for Adolescents
Chicago, IL: 800-621-3860

Chemical Referral Center
Washington, D.C.:   800-262-8200

Child Abuse Hotline (National)
Woodland Hills, CA: 800-422-4453

Drug Abuse Information and Referral Line,
National Institute on Drug Abuse
Rockville, MD: 800-662-4357

Hearing and Speech Action, National Association

Rockville, MD: 800-638-8255

Juvenile Diabetes Foundation International
New York, NY: 800-223-1138

Missing Children Help Center
Tampa, FL :   800-872-5437

Missing Children Network
Dayton, OH: 800-235-5906

Mothers Against Drunk Driving
Hurst, TX: 800-438-6233

Narcotics Education
Washington, D.C.:   800-548-8700

National Federation of Parents for Drug Free Youth
Silver Spring, MD: 800-554-5437

National Adolescent Suicide Hotline
Chicago, IL: 800-621-4000

National Down's Syndrome Congress
Park Ridge, IL: 800-232-6372

National Hotline for Missing Children
Washington, D.C.:   800-843-5678

Pride/National Parents Resource Institute for
Drug Education
Atlanta, GA: 800-241-7946

Reyes Syndrome Foundation National
Bryan, OH: 800-233-7393

Runaway Hotline
Austin, TX: (U.S, except Texas)   800-231-6946
                                         (Texas)   800-392-3352

Notes

Notes

Notes

Notes

Buy two, get one free!

Each of our handbook series (LIFESTYLE, COMMUNICATION, PRODUCTIVITY, and LEADERSHIP) was designed to give you the most comprehensive collection of hands-on desktop references all related to a specific topic. They're a great value at the regular price of $12.95 ($14.95 in Canada); plus, at the unbeatable offer of buy two at the regular price and get one free, you can't find a better value in learning resources. **To order**, see the back of this page for the entire handbook selection.

1. Fill out and send the entire page by mail to:

National Press Publications
6901 West 63rd Street
P.O. Box 2949
Shawnee Mission, Kansas 66201-1349

2. Or **FAX 1-913-432-0824**

3. Or call toll-free **1-800-258-7248** (**1-800-685-4142** in Canada)

Fill out completely:

Name _____
Organization _____
Address _____
City _____
State/Province _____ ZIP/Postal Code _____
Telephone ( ) _____

Method of Payment:

☐ Enclosed is my check or money order

☐ Please charge to:

    ☐ MasterCard   ☐ VISA   ☐ American Express

Signature _____ Exp. Date _____
Credit Card Number
☐ ☐ ☐ ☐ ☐ ☐ ☐ ☐ ☐ ☐ ☐ ☐ ☐

To order multiple copies for co-workers and friends: U.S. Can.
20-50 copies..$8.50 $10.95
More than 50 copies..$7.50 $ 9.95

VIP# 705-008486-093

OTHER DESKTOP HANDBOOKS

	Qty	Item#	Title	U.S.	Can.	Total
LEADERSHIP		410	The Supervisor's Handbook, Revised and Expanded	$12.95	$14.95	
		418	Total Quality Management	$12.95	$14.95	
		421	Change: Coping with Tomorrow Today	$12.95	$14.95	
		458	Positive Performance Management *A Guide to Win-Win Reviews*	$12.95	$14.95	
		459	Techniques of Successful Delegation	$12.95	$14.95	
		463	Powerful Leadership Skills for Women	$12.95	$14.95	
		494	Team-Building	$12.95	$14.95	
		495	How to Manage Conflict	$12.95	$14.95	
		469	Peak Performance	$12.95	$14.95	
COMMUNICATION		413	Dynamic Communication Skills for Women	$12.95	$14.95	
		414	The Write Stuff: *A Style Manual for Effective Business Writing*	$12.95	$14.95	
		417	Listen Up: *Hear What's Really Being Said*	$12.95	$14.95	
		442	Assertiveness: *Get What You Want Without Being Pushy*	$12.95	$14.95	
		460	Techniques to Improve Your Writing Skills	$12.95	$14.95	
		461	Powerful Presentation Skills	$12.95	$14.95	
		482	Techniques of Effective Telephone Communication	$12.95	$14.95	
		485	Personal Negotiating Skills	$12.95	$14.95	
		488	Customer Service: *The Key to Winning Lifetime Customers*	$12.95	$14.95	
		498	How to Manage Your Boss	$12.95	$14.95	
PRODUCTIVITY		411	Getting Things Done: *An Achiever's Guide to Time Management*	$12.95	$14.95	
		443	A New Attitude	$12.95	$14.95	
		468	Understanding the Bottom Line: *Finance for the Non-Financial Manager*	$12.95	$14.95	
		483	Successful Sales Strategies: *A Woman's Perspective*	$12.95	$14.95	
		489	Doing Business Over the Phone *Telemarketing for the '90s*	$12.95	$14.95	
		496	Motivation & Goal-Setting *The Keys to Achieving Success*	$12.95	$14.95	
LIFESTYLE		415	Balancing Career & Family: *Overcoming the Superwoman Syndrome*	$12.95	$14.95	
		416	Real Men Don't Vacuum	$12.95	$14.95	
		464	Self-Esteem: *The Power to Be Your Best*	$12.95	$14.95	
		484	The Stress Management Handbook	$12.95	$14.95	
		486	Parenting: *Ward & June Don't Live Here Anymore*	$12.95	$14.95	
		487	How to Get the Job You Want	$12.95	$14.95	

SALES TAX All purchases subject to state and local sales tax. Questions? Call **1-800-258-7248**		
	Subtotal	
	Sales Tax (Add appropriate state and local tax)	
	Shipping and Handling ($1 one item, 50¢ each additional item)	
	Total	

VIP#705-008486-093